I0814463

The Lombards in Italy

PAST IMPERFECT

Further Information and Publications

www.arc-humanities.org/series/book-series/

The Lombards in Italy

Christopher Heath

British Library Cataloguing in Publication Data

A catalogue record for this book is available from the British Library.

ISBN (print) 9781802702699
e-ISBN (PDF) 9781802704280
e-ISBN (EPUB) 9781802704297

www.arc-humanities.org

Printed and bound in the UK (by CPIGroup [UK] Ltd), USA (by Bookmasters), and elsewhere using print-on-demand technology.

Publisher (manufacturer) details: Arc Humanities Press, 14 Clifton Moor Business Village, James Nicolson Link, York YO30 4XG, United Kingdom.

EU Authorized Representative details (for GPSR purposes): Amsterdam University Press, Nieuwe Prinsengracht 89, 1018 VR Amsterdam, The Netherlands. www.aup.nl

Contents

List of Illustrations

Preface and Acknowledgements

This book discusses the Lombards in Italy from their first appearance in the northeast of the peninsula towards the third quarter of the sixth century until the end of their political structures in the South, over six hundred years later. Along the way we shall discuss, not only their structures of governance and their rulers, but also their enduring impact on Italian history and culture. As we shall see this is not an entirely familiar story, but nonetheless a fascinating and evocative testimony of the solutions and responses of one group to the problems and realities of a post-Roman landscape.

It is important at this initial stage to make a remark on terminology. A careful reader will note, in what follows, that both the terms "Lombards" and "Langobards" will be used interchangeably. Strictly speaking, the correct term is "Langobards" taken from the origin stories of the Lombards which we will meet below. However, akin to other Anglosphere terms, "Lombard" and Lombards have become entrenched in Anglophone scholarship and discourse. It should not, however, be assumed that Lombardy (the modern region of Lombardia) is commensurate with the old kingdom since the Lombards ruled practically most of northern and central Italy and subsequently mainland southern Italy.

My own authorial journey to this point has also traversed a lengthy journey helped along the way by friends and colleagues who have either responded to specific enquiries, assisted with bibliographical enquiries or provided feedback to early draft material. Let me mention specifically, Dr. Clemens Gantner, Dr. Edoardo Manarini, Tom Sossic, and William Curtis for their help and friendship, Professor Paul Fouracre and Professor Jamie Wood for their guidance and advice, but above all Dr. Bojana Radovanović for her assistance, elegance, love, and care. It is to her that I dedicate this book. Naturally, all errors remain mine, but without their help the book would be much weaker. In writing, I remain enthused by the example of Thomas Hodgkin whose prodigious output produced *Italy and Her Invaders* which in its own way propelled me on my own lengthy journey one cold winter's day in Manchester some years ago.

Christopher Heath
Levenshulme, May 2025
cheath@lincoln.ac.uk

Glossary

aldius/aldia	A male or female individual who is "half-free" subject to some restrictions on their personal freedom. Equated to the *servi ministeriales* in the *Edictum Rothari*.
angargathungi	"According to rank"; the key principle behind Lombard law which was based on calibrated *gwidrigilds*, i.e., wergilds.
gastald	A local official, in the kingdom dependent upon Pavia for authority, but in Benevento, particularly, from the ninth century an official who acted as the local ruler regardless of either princely or comital authority.
marpahis	"Master of the horse"; one of the significant court positions of Lombard kings and dukes in Benevento.
mundoald	The male family member (usually) who held the *mundium* of his female relatives, be that wife, sister, or daughter, and thus protected her interests in law.
schultheis	The local judge through whom the Lombard kings governed and adjudicated.
stolesayz	An official at the Lombard courts who may be equated to the treasurer.

Introduction

A trip into any mainstream bookshop in Britain will reveal that so far as booksellers are concerned Italian history commences with the Renaissance. Naturally, one also finds many works on the Roman Empire, and particularly the Principate (i.e., 27 BCE–68 CE), but the best part of a thousand years of Italian life and experience are left uncovered. Beyond Britain and the commercial world of booksellers, however, a vibrant community of scholars has spent the last half-century or so engaging with and putting to bed old shibboleths of hordes, of decline and fall, of impulsive sword-and-sandal protagonists, and all the usual impedimenta associated with so-called "barbarians." The centrality of Late Antiquity and the Early Middle Ages to fundamental aspects of the modern world makes study and engagement of that time and period both important and compelling.

The Lombards have long formed part of that world. They allegedly embody the perfect exemplification of "barbarians": crude, uncouth, violent and, usually, pagan. The great Italian historian of the eighteenth-century Ludovico Antonio Muratori (1672–1750) summed up this view: "they were barbarians, and that's that" (*erano barbari e tanto basta*). The debate that flowed throughout the eighteenth and the nineteenth centuries pivoted around the subject of Romans and barbarians. The *questione longobarda* pivoted around the (mainly Italian) debate about the contribution or role of the Lombards to Italian civilization and culture. How could the world of Augustus (27 BCE–14 CE), Cicero (106 BCE–43 BCE), and Sallust (86 BCE–ca. 35 BCE) fall prey to the ill-disciplined and the illiterate who, as Sidonius Apollinaris (ca. 430–81/90 CE) pointedly remarked, applied rancid butter to their hair? In this reading, the Lombards—the archetypical barbarians—simply by their irruption into Italy propelled most of the peninsula into a time of ruin, involution, and decay. There is, however, much more of value to consider. In recent discussions of the Early Medieval world, much work has been done to engage with a more positive evaluation of the centuries after Rome and, importantly, on the terms of the period itself.

This book seeks to redress this gap and engage with the fascinating world of the Lombards in Italy who contributed to the political, social, and economic life of the peninsula for over six hundred years. This may be an unfamiliar Italy to some readers, but it is one that is much more than simply a degraded and dismal epilogue to Roman Italy or even an obscure prologue for the development of communal Italy in the central Middle Ages. This book travels across a lengthy chronological period; it commences the story of the Lombards in the far northeast of modern Italy and moves, for the final chapter, to the far south of the current republic. In between can be found discussions of kings, dukes, popes, and emperors, but it also seeks to engage with the real quotidian lives of those who were or who identified themselves as Lombards. It is an evocative journey that reflects in many ways upon the common experiences of many parts of Europe after the Roman Empire.

Whilst academic contact with the world of the Lombards has increased and improved in the Anglophone sphere, recent synthetic works in English remain relatively rare. Recent studies which position the Lombards within their remit are affected by their core treatment. Chris Wickham's 1981 work *Early Medieval Italy* is now forty-four years old, and whilst it has stood the test of time remarkably well, it never held the Lombards as the core point of discussion given that the work runs from 400–1000. Similarly, Neil

Christie's work *The Lombards: The Ancient Longobards*, whilst maintaining the Lombards at the centre of a mainly material culture discussion, provides limited commentary on their activities post-568 and, for all intents and purposes, residual comment post-774. The edited volume, *Italy in the Early Middle Ages*, also maintains a wider remit than the Lombards alone, and is strong on subjects other than the traditional geopolitical narratives. Whilst this book is close to twenty years old now and still useful, the centrality of discussion is focused on Italy as a geographical construct, and thus the Lombards play second fiddle. Finally, the edited volume *The Langobards before the Frankish Conquest*, which deliberately ends in 774, is a useful update to earlier scholarship but is rather specialized in format and presentation, representing (as is common for the series in which it stands) an article and discussion (in Spoleto style) which is aimed at a rigorously academic audience. Nonetheless, all these works still retain much of interest and value and will be useful for those readers who want to delve further into the Lombard world. Finally, the eminent work of Thomas Hodgkin (1831–1913), the multi-volume *Italy and Her Invaders* is perhaps rather dated but is still robust after over a century, and it remains useful, as do the pertinent chapters in the *New Cambridge Medieval History*, although for the first volume (edited by Paul Fouracre), there is not an independent chapter on the Lombards (as he laments). Let us start our discussion of the Lombards by reverting to their infrequent appearances in classical texts before they attained sight of *il bel paese*.

A Journey from the Elbe

For nearly the entire duration of the Roman Empire in the west, the *Langobardi* were a distant and insignificant group of barbarians subject to the shifting sands of heterogeneous confederations of peoples formed to resist the heavy hand of Roman imperialism. Their intermittent appearances in Roman historical ethnography were infrequent, meagre, and, for us, problematic.[1] Notices to them only appear in four narratives, all separated by time, treatment, and conception. Taken collectively, these notices are problematic because it is unsafe to assume that the *Langobardi* of the time of Velleius Paterculus (ca. 19 BCE–31 CE) were directly linked to the *Langobardi* who crossed the Alps with Alboin (ca. 565–572) into Italy in 568/9. Whilst this short book keeps the Lombards in Italy as its principal theme, brief consideration of the Lombards' transit from the north to the Mediterranean will aid our understanding of their pre-historical legacy. That legacy remained fundamental to their own developed conception of identity when resident in Italy. This transit across most of Europe will also prompt questions about the significance of the Lombards in any study of Early Medieval Europe, which will also be addressed below. But before this is done, let us return to Velleius Paterculus.

Velleius served with the future Emperor Tiberius (14–37 CE) in Germania and thus has the rather unusual distinction for a commentator on matters "barbarian" to actually have had direct knowledge of his subject matter. His *History*, however, has been rather undervalued by commentators, who were unimpressed by his rhetoric and hyperbole. Frederick Shipley (1871–1945), who prepared the Loeb edition, thought that a compendium "hastily compiled could hardly be expected to rise to the level of great history or great literature."[2] Velleius's comments on the Lombards pitch us immediately into an issue we shall encounter when discussing the Lombards in Italy. In describing the generalship of Tiberius, Velleius indicated that "the power of the *Langobardi* was broken, [they were] a race surpassing even the Germans in savagery" (*fracti Langobardi, gens etiam Germana feritate fero-*

1 Pliny the Elder's (23/4–79) twenty-volume *Bella Germaniae* is lost. So too, the *Libri Belli Germanici* of Aufidius Bassus (*fl.* ca. 30–ca. 60) whose work Pliny had continued. Tacitus may have used both authors for his *Germania*.

2 *Velleius Paterculus: Compendium of Roman History*, ed. F. W. Shipley (Cambridge: Harvard University Press, 1924).

cior).[3] Successful military leaders are not generally known to defeat gentle enemies, and whilst the concept of *feritas* had assumed a standard attribution for the "Germans," and may have resulted from the use of predictable commonplaces (as Woodman remarks), there is no specific reason for doubting the report of Velleius, even though it helps to adorn his account of the military successes of his patron.[4]

The Lombards next appear in Strabo's (63/4 BCE–24 CE) multi-volume masterpiece, the *Geographica*, which provided a descriptive ethnography of peoples and places of Europe, Asia, and Africa. Strabo was well travelled but does not himself suggest that he ventured north of the Alps. Even so, it is more than likely that he had reliable sources of information. He tells us that the *Langobardi* (*ΓαΥκόβαροί*) were part of the Suevi and dwelt on the far side of the Elbe (*Albis*). He adds that the *Langobardi* had been "driven to flight out of their country into the land on the far side of the river."[5] Beyond this, Strabo simply highlights the alleged ease with which the peoples of this part of the world would migrate because of their temporary dwellings, viewing them as essentially nomads. Akin to Strabo, our third commentator, Tacitus (ca. 56–ca. 120 CE) also associated the *Langobardi* with the Suevi. He introduces a comment on them that is echoed nearly eight centuries later by Paul the Deacon. They are famous, he tells us, "because they are so few. Hemmed in as they are by many mighty peoples, they find safety, not in submission but in facing the risks of battle."[6] It remains doubtful, however, that the comments of Tacitus, here specifically or more broadly in his *Germania*, should hold great weight in terms of

3 *Velleius Paterculus*, 2.106.

4 *Velleuis Paterculus: The Tiberian Narrative (2.94–131)*, ed. A. J. Woodman (Cambridge University Press, 2004), 143.

5 Strabo, *Geography*, ed. Horace Leonard Jones (Harvard University Press, 1989), 7:1.3.

6 Tacitus, *The Agricola and The Germania*, ed. H. Mattingly (Penguin, 1948), xl.

historical reliability.[7] Given the rather brief remarks provided (albeit within a wider context), we are only now seized of two essential traits that might be linked to the Lombards: that is their limitation in numerical strength and their apparent bellicosity in war.

The final of our four commentators within the tradition of Romano-Greek historical ethnography was Cassius Dio (ca. 165–ca. 235 CE). Dio's *Roman History* of eighty books (of which about twenty-six survive complete) was written in Greek and ran from the time of Aeneas (notionally ca. 1100 BCE) up to 229 CE. Whilst Dio travelled westwards from his home province of Bithynia in Asia Minor, the closest he may have got to the *Langobardi* was during his time as proconsul in Pannonia. Whether one doubts the utility of Cassius Dio or not, his remarks on the *Langobardi* relate to 168 CE an ill-fated rout of the *Obii* and the *Langobardi* as they crossed the Danube (*Ister*) within the context of the Marcommanic Wars (166–180 CE).[8] This reference appears to be the first notice to the Lombards at some distance from their Elbe homelands, but it is probably too early to suggest that they had already commenced their transit south-eastwards. It is, nonetheless, the first hint of significant shifts in the settlement landscapes of territories beyond the Roman Empire. For the Lombards, it is the last notice we have of their activities, which then remain unrecorded until the fifth century.

Into this gap one may consider the witness of later Lombard and Frankish sources. Whilst history, legend, and archaeology are not happy bedfellows, the traditions set out by Paul the Deacon in his *Historia Langobardorum*, the *Origo gentis Langobardorum* (hereafter *OgL*), the curious and unique *Historia Langobardorum codicis Gothani* (hereafter

---

7 Richard F. Thomas, "The Germania as Literary Text," in *The Cambridge Companion to Tacitus*, ed. A. J. Woodman (Cambridge University Press, 2010), 59–72.

8 Cassius Dio, *Roman History*, ed. Ernest Cary (Harvard University Press, 1989), 72.

HLcG), and even Fredegar in "his" historical compendium shed light on how the Lombards themselves, at different moments, perceived their origins. We are cast into an ahistorical world of Gods, Amazons, and heroes, where historians should fear to tread.

Even so, taking the *OgL* as the original version (which is somewhat controversial), we read that the *Langobardi* were given their name by Godan/Woden, and the *OgL* explains how this occurred: Originally, the *Langobardi* had been called the *Winnili*s (or *Winniles*, which might mean "the fighters"[9]) and lived on an island called *Scandanan*, which was in northern parts (*in partibus aquilonis*) where many peoples dwelt. The *Winnili*, however, were a "small people," subject to a demand for tribute by the Vandals, who declared: "Either pay us tributes or prepare yourselves for battle and fight with us."[10] The leaders of the *Winnili*, Ybor and Agio, galvanized by their mother, Gambara, decided that "it is better for us to make ready the battle than to pay tributes to the Vandals." Both peoples then sought the aid of the Gods. Godan responded to the Vandals that whoever he saw first at sunrise would be given the victory. Meanwhile, the *Winnili* leaders were advised by Frea/Freyr that their "women, with their hair let down around the face in the likeness of a beard should also come with their husbands." When the sun was rising, Frea turned Godan's bed to face the *Winnili* and their women. "Who are these Long-beards?" (*langobardae*) asked Godan. "As you have given them a name, give them also the victory," responded Frea. Thus, thereafter, the *Winnili* were called Langobards. Both Fredegar and Paul the Deacon recount their own, slightly variant iterations of this story. For the latter, in the first book of the *Historia Langobardorum* (hereafter *HL*),

9 *Italian Carolingian Historical and Poetic Texts*, ed. Luigi Andrea Berto (Pisa University Press, 2016), 52n10.

10 *History of the Langobards*, ed. Foulke, 327. Where a short-form in-text citation is provided as an initial reference, please consult the Further Reading at the end for further details.

however, these events were simply a "silly fable" (*ridicula fabula*) and worthy of laughter; the "fable" should "be held of no account."[11] Using a combination of erudite euhemerism and etymological sleight-of-hand, Paul the Deacon explained the real origins. It was, he pointed out, simply due to the long beards of the *Winnili* which were left "untouched by the knife" and "Wotan" (Godan) had existed "not about these times, but long before and not in Germany but in Greece." Whilst the details of the origin myth are fascinating and reflect (partially) the classical ethnographic idea that the Langobards were a small group in a sea of shifting tribal confederations, the striking feature here is the longevity of the story itself. It still retained resonance in terms of identity-formation for the Lombards in the eighth century, even though the Lombards had long turned away from any active form of Paganism. At best, however, it does demonstrate an interest in their deep past by elite individuals and commentators, though it would be a mistake to elevate the interest into anything more than that. The twin pillars of identity and religion, like all peoples in the early medieval west, were fundamental for the Lombards, and we shall return to this subject in Chapter Three. For now, however, it remains significant that as entirely catholic and orthodox a commentator as Paul the Deacon did not evidently feel able to excise the *riducula fabula* from his *HL*.

Later historians have also used these origin stories as evidence of the persistence of a particular approach to identity by some of the elite of the Lombards in the seventh century, assuming that the *OgL*, in particular, was attached physically to the newly minted *Edictum Rothari* (hereafter *ER*) of 643.[12] The northern and pagan ambience of the origin story excited much comment amongst a wide array of

---

11 The edition of the *HL* used here is *History of the Langobards*, ed. Foulke; hereafter it will be cited parenthetically in the text by book and chapter number.

12 The most accessible edition is *The Lombard Laws*, ed. Drew; hereafter this will be cited parenthetically by page number.

historians during the nineteenth and twentieth centuries, both north and south of the Alps. It became entangled into broader discussions that circulated around (usually) a binary paradigm, where Romans and Germans operated as the principal engine for historical comment on change in Late Antiquity and the Early Middle Ages. In this reading, the *OgL*, the account of Fredegar, or Paul the Deacon's retelling could all demonstrate the "barbarian" quality of the Lombards. They could then assume all the usual pejorative attributes imagined and real for groups that moved into and adopted rule of former parts of the Roman Empire. Historians could adduce the reports of the classical ethnographers discussed above, add the remarks of Prokopios about one Lombard group whom the Byzantine *generalissimo* Narses (ca. 478/80–ca. 566/73) could not control, and mix into this the eschatological fears of Pope Gregory the Great (590–604), who feared their "barbarity." In mixing all these elements together, the Lombards were generated as the prime laboratory example of an uncivilized and savage people who erupted into the civilized Italy. Their appearance in Italy could be depicted as an alien exception and violent intrusion. Giovanni Tabacco (1914–2002), in his influential *The Struggle for Power in Medieval Italy*, suggests that the advent of the Lombards caused a "profound upheaval of all social relationships."[13] To be fair to Tabacco, however, his commentary follows on from a lengthy historiographical tradition that may be traced back as far as Niccolò Machiavelli (1469–1527). Here, we do not have the space to detail all the responses of commentators to the Lombards specifically or to "barbarians" generally. It is nonetheless worthwhile to consider the broad and influential impulses behind nineteenth and twentieth century scholarship which may help in understanding the relative neglect that the Lombards as a subject have experienced.

13 Giovanni Tabacco, *The Struggle for Power in Medieval Italy: Structures of Political Rule* (Cambridge University Press, 1989), 95.

Abstractions that pigeon-hole this or that ethnic group as "barbarian" or "civilized" are not fundamentally useful ways to view the Lombards in Italy or, more broadly, the socio-political entities that followed on from the Roman Empire in the west. Barbarism is and was a subjective category. As will be discussed in following chapters (particularly Chapter Four), it isn't a helpful way through the thicket of evidence that we may use to discuss the settlement of the Lombards in Italy or to address the evident complexity on the ground. This perspective may be corrected when considered in comparison to the Lombards' contemporaries. It is important to emphasize that the Lombards can correct the perspective that used this historiographical categorization. Like the Franks in Gaul and the Anglo-Saxons in Britain, their settlement into Italy was not undertaken with a "slash-and-burn" approach that rendered their new homes into an early medieval *tabula rasa*. One group did not simply replace the entire autochthonous population and start again from scratch. The Lombards, who were often said to be the embodiment of the nail-in-the-coffin of Roman civilization, stand as a people who developed a new synthesis of Lombard and Roman which deployed an effective settlement strategy. That strategy encompassed the whole population of early medieval Italy. We shall see this clearly in Chapter Two, which discusses the physical and human space into which the Lombards entered.

Before we approach the borders of Italy, however, we should return to the Lombards, who between the Marcommanic Wars and their advent into Italy appear to have moved south and eastwards from their origins in the far north of modern Germany. However, joining the dots between their *ur-heimat* and their new Mediterranean home is difficult to achieve with any certainty. The later witness of Paul the Deacon (in the first book of the *HL*) reports movement from obscure areas called *Mauringa* to *Golanda* and onwards further to *Anthaib*, *Banthaib*, and *Vurgundaib*. As Christie pointed out, it is not possible to identify each point or acquire any absolute sense of chronology attained. We may consider the general idea that the Langobards were settled in what is now modern-day Bohemia between ca. 460 and ca. 480. If we are to believe the anonymous author of the later ninth-century *HLcG*, when Odovacar (ca. 433–493) moved against and defeated the Rugians of Feletheus (475–487) in 487, the Lombards moved into "Rugiland" (broadly modern Niederösterreich, i.e., the left bank of the Danube between Linz and Wien), which was adjacent to land occupied by the Heruls. It is from this point onwards that we may have greater certainty about both the historical existence and activity of the Lombards, albeit from commentators separated by either chronology or geography; they are no longer temporally uneven or spatially uncertain.

Since the Lombards were the neighbours of the Heruls, they became entangled within the web of Byzantine diplomacy on the Middle Danube, and they once again become the subject matter of external comment. Both Prokopios (490–565) and Paul the Deacon recount how the Lombards under King Tato (ca. 500–ca. 510) fought and vanquished the Heruls at some point around 508, and were thus secure in their occupation of an area which Paul the Deacon called *Feld*. This area may represent the Wienviertel in modern Niederösterreich. Waccho (ca. 510–540) both supplanted and killed Tato and defeated Tato's son, Hildechis to cement his rule. Waccho, Paul tells us, had three wives. The second of these had two daughters: Wisegarda (ca. 510–ca. 540), who married Theudebert I, King of the Franks (533–548), and Walderada (531–572), who also married the Frankish King "Cusupald" (Theudebald 547/8–555), who then "gave her" to one of his followers, Garibald I of Bavaria (555–591). Whilst interesting, these details demonstrate the formation of a complex series of alliance systems that were modelled on the earlier so-called *Ehepolitik* of King Theoderic the Great (489–526), which for Waccho provided protection on the western side of Lombard territory but also enhanced his prestige and the power of the Lombard kings. Meanwhile, the Lombards could concentrate on meeting the challenge represented by the Gepids to the southeast of their lands. Prokopios and Paul the Deacon note that the Lombards moved into Pannonia under

Audoin (546–ca. 565), although the former indicates that it was Justinian (527–565) who "gave them" this land (together with considerable subsidies) as a proxy force to counter the Gepids. Across several years, both Lombards and Gepids fought against each other, probably encouraged by Justinian's connivance, as he played one group against another. In 551/2, however, the Gepid army was defeated. After the death of Audoin, his son Alboin agreed a "perpetual treaty with the Avars" and reduced the Gepids to "utter destruction" (*HL* 1.23, 1.27). Subsequently, Alboin "bestowed his own abode...Pannonia" upon the Avars, and the Lombards left for Italy (*HL* 2.7).

Undoubtedly, the Lombards, the original *Winnili*, were entirely transformed in the centuries between their encounters with the army of Tiberius and their final defeat of the Gepids, but in what ways may remain beyond historical enquiry and stand within the stimulating world of archaeological discovery. Whether Alboin and his followers were aware of the lengthy and uncertain travails of their people as they stood on the threshold of Italy is not known, but it is perhaps unlikely that he or his people would have expected or predicted their enduring legacy to Italy and the Italians. Let us now turn to what the Lombards encountered next once their crossed the Dinaric Alps.

Chapter I

Space: Climate and Physical Environments

Physical Contexts

Italy is neither a uniform climate zone nor a homogenous settlement area. Climatic and geographical variance was further reflected by the political disunity that the Lombards are said to have created. However, this overemphasizes the impact of the Lombards on a collation of societies that were fundamentally local in their orientation and management. Notwithstanding the fact that the north of Italy had been part and parcel of the Roman Empire for over seven centuries, the tapestry of plains, mountains, foothills, rivers, and coasts rendered the peninsula into an interconnected but also disconnected set of provinces and cities. Italy is (and was), of course, framed by three key elements: first, the Alps to the north encircles the north Italian Po plain; second, the Apennines running across and down the spine of the peninsula, which restricted straightforward communication from the Adriatic littoral to the opposite Tuscan coasts; and, finally, the entire peninsula is deeply affected by its Mediterranean coasts, which remained fundamental in terms of communication throughout the Early Middle Ages. These broad characteristics necessarily simplify the complexity of landscapes and conditions on the ground. The Lombard Kingdom was principally associated with the Po plain, but even here it did not control the full extent of the river and the riverine system(s). Likewise, it held portions of the Alpine and pre-Alps areas, but the Franks retained control of the Val d'Aosta in this period and thus a crucial gateway across and into Italy. Further south, the Kingdom controlled the northern portion of modern Tuscany and the uplands of modern Umbria around Spoleto, which in turn abutted the Beneventan province. The latter displayed a wide array of physical geographical variance. The Lombard *Mezzogiorno* (a later but useful term), encompassed its own variety, from upland and mountainous zones to riverine and coastal plains. The Apennines dominated the central spine of the south and stretched into Calabria. Even the coastal plains here are narrow in places, and cultivation was thus limited by topography.

There is also significant variance in terms of climate. Whilst the entire peninsula has a temperate Mediterranean climate, Italy may be divided into four broad zones: first, on the islands and in the south of Italy, a climate regime of hot summers and mild winters; second, to the north, an area of warm summers and mild winters which varies in terms of altitude (an important caveat for the High Apennines); third, and further north again, the Po valley, which is hot in summer, cold in winter, and wet in both spring and autumn; and, finally, an Alpine climate in the mountainous Alpine and Apennine districts. Yet it is important not to view climate as a static system that is not subject to dynamic changes; both short- and long-term adjustments can and do occur. In the period under discussion here, several hypothetical variances occurred in the Mediterranean. After the so-called Roman warm period between ca. 250 BCE and 400 CE, a wetter climate, also called the Late Antique Ice Age (ca. 500–ca. 700, sometimes exactly calibrated to 536–660) affected Italy. Some commentators have linked these colder and wetter conditions to the global impact of three large volcanic eruptions in 535/6, 539/40, and 547. The first of these prompted a century-long global temperature decline which may have amounted to as much as 2°C.[1] There are narrative references to both extraor-

1 Ulf Büntgen et al., "Cooling and Societal Change During the Late Antique Little Ice Age from 536 to Around 660 AD," *Nature Geoscience* 9 (2016): 231–36.

dinary inundations and poor crop yields caused by the lack of sunshine and pleasant weather.[2] While one must be careful not to develop circular arguments and extrapolation from anecdotal materials in narrative sources, this period, in terms of economic activity, also marks the nadir of trade and wealth in the broader Mediterranean. One can see an involution in trans-regional connections and longer-distance trade, but at the same time a re-focusing of local and intra-peninsular activity which in some respects also maintained links to Constantinople and beyond. Subsequently, the peninsula entered the medieval warm period, which ran from 900 to 1200. This was also congruent with deeper economic activity and the development of trade networks across the whole of the Mediterranean. Still, one does not necessarily prompt the other, although it may be theorized that, over the long term, population levels and thus economic demand increased. Looking at the specific contexts, however, will permit insight into the processes on the ground and how the Lombards and Lombard society managed the physical challenges they encountered.

As much as forty percent of Italy is mountainous. The Apennines extend from the tip of (modern) Calabria all the way to their junction with the Ligurian Alps, a total distance of one thousand two hundred kilometres to the north. In turn, they may be divided into Northern, Central and Southern chains, and they offer different pathways across and between the western and eastern sides of the land. As Figure 1 demonstrates, the mountainous imprint of the peninsula frames the human contexts in terms of both landscape use and human habitation. Given this mountainous imprint, rivers and plains assume a greater significance in terms of fertility. One may isolate four low-level plains controlled by the Lombards in this period. First, the Po valley as the heartland of the Kingdom was of primordial importance, although the Kingdom did not command the estuary of the river; second, in *Tuscia*, the Arno

2 Karin Zonneveld et al., "Climate Change, Society, and Pandemic Disease in Roman Italy Between 200BCE and 600CE," *Science Advances* 10 (2024): 1–11.

Figure 1. Physical relief map of Italy. Map by Eric Gaba (Sting) and NordNordWest. Wikimedia Commons. CC BY-SA 3.0.

valley and its linked rivers; third, parts of Campania, although this was contested with Naples; and fourth, the plains of Puglia. As Marco Panato shows in his *River and Society in Northern Italy: The Po Valley 500–1000* management of the fluvial networks was crucial to the economic health of the Lombard Kingdom. Long-distance trade continued to use the Po and its tributaries in this period. Legal titles in the laws of Liutprand

and Ratchis regulated merchants according to their wealth. Aside from the highest mountains and marshland, however, pre-Lombard Italy was a landscape deeply affected by a human imprint.

Human Contexts

The Lombards did not inherit an empty landscape. Italy had been fashioned, crafted, and managed by humans for millennia prior to their arrival. Perhaps the clearest imprint that remained for them, however, would have been the Roman rule of the peninsula, which had been in place for well over a thousand years in parts of central Italy and over half that in what was known as *Gallia Cisalpina*.

We have already noted the climatic and environmental disunities but mapped onto these should be human divisions, which add further layers of complexity. Augustus (27 BCE–14 CE) divided Italy into eleven regions (excluding Corsica, Sardinia, and Sicily), which were reorganized during the rule of Diocletian (284–305), who created a *Dioecesis Italiciana* including all of modern Italy together with Corsica and *Rhaetia* (broadly modern Switzerland). Later, the *Diocesis* was further divided into *Italia annonaria* and *suburbicaria*. The physical unity of the peninsula, however, endured in the minds of commentators. The provincial digest that Paul the Deacon intrudes as a digression into his *HL* suggests that this remained the case in the eighth century. Paul lists eighteen provinces of Italy, including Sardinia, Corsica, and Sicily. His regional digest is based upon Augustan provincial designations with several interpolated inventions of his own. This is interesting because it signals a persistence of a conceptual understanding of Italy as the whole peninsula together with the adjacent islands. Lombard Italy was never coterminous with the whole of the old Italian Roman diocese. Indeed, Lombard Italy was not a static entity at all in terms of spatial control. Alboin's initial conquests were essentially restricted to the northern Po plains and across to the Alps. Through the later part of the sixth century and up to the time of Rothari

Figure 2. Map of Italy in the early seventh century. Map created by TCI Cartographic Office for the Italian Encyclopedia of Giovanni Treccani Institute. Wikipedia. Courtesy of the Touring Club Italiano. CC BY-SA 4.0.

(636–652), Lombard domains were consolidated in this northern zone, with independent settlement in *Tuscia*, Spoleto, and Benevento (see Figure 2). Across the next century or so, further gains were made at the expense of the Empire in the north, centre, and south of the peninsula. The Lombards nibbled away at the edges of Imperial territory both in the south and in the north. More dramatic, at some point (perhaps ca. 700) the Lombards added Corsica to their dominions. Aistulf (749–756) definitively extinguished the Exarchate of Ravenna in 751, which left only vestigial mainland remnants of the Empire around the Venetian lagoon, Rome, Naples, and Otranto. With the end of the Kingdom in the north in 774, the Lombard zone was refocused on the south and centred on Benevento, which for the next seventy years encompassed most of the modern *Mezzogiorno*. As we shall see in Chapter Five, *Langobardia minor* would divide politically into several competing Lombard polities who were in active competition with the local mercantile elites of Naples, Amalfi, and Gaeta but also engaged with significant Islamic settlement and polities based on Bari, Taranto, and Agropoli. The famous appearance of Norman mercenaries in Salerno in 999 commenced the last phase of Lombard rule, where progressively over the next eighty years the Lombard elites were co-opted and then rendered obsolete by the Normans, who turned themselves into the new masters of southern Italy.

Population levels are always difficult to estimate in this period. It is, however, worth the effort because they permit some understanding of the basic underpinning of economic demand at any given point in time, and by implication suggest the viability of trade both in regional and trans-regional terms. The population total may have been 2.4 million in 600, rising to five million by 1000. However, a more recent estimate by Shane Bobrycki elevates the figure to eight million, remaining stable from 600 to 800, as mortality pressures such as war and plague declined. In terms of densities, however, these may have been modest as an average across the landscape, with obvious concentrations in cities such as Pavia, Milan, and Verona.

Given the irregularity of the rural environment, it is difficult to make specific extrapolations concerning village populations that would operate in all regions of Lombard Italy. Christie observed that where Lombard rural sites had been attested archaeologically, they seemed to favour higher ground. In some localities a significant caesura in settlement occurs across the fifth and sixth centuries. On the one hand, in modern Tuscany there is evidence for the continuous survival of hilltop villages, and similar developments may be identified in the modern region of *Piemonte* (Piedmont) in the northeast. Discerning whether these settlements were primarily sited for defensive purposes is problematic. A case in point is the settlement of Belmonte in the Sabina, where archaeological investigations uncovered both agricultural and military metalwork. It is not unreasonable to envisage mixed use for these sites, dependent, again, upon the local conditions that prevailed.

The Rural Space

The popular work of Giulio Cesare Croce (1550–1609), *Le sottilissime astutie di Bertoldo*, recounts the mythical life of Bertoldo at the court of Alboin in either Verona or Pavia. This work was followed by *Le piacevoli et ridicolose simplicità di Bertoldino*, which dealt with the son of Bertoldo and his amusing simplicity. Whilst the context of these stories is fictional, they remind us that Lombard Italy was an agricultural society. Dig just a little beneath the surface of the Lombard laws, for instance, and one will find a set of regulations that organize and protect the rural and agricultural rhythms of the year. Modern analysis of agrarian life and praxis in early medieval Italy has moved on from the work of Emilio Sereni and his *History of the Italian Agricultural Landscape*, which used a limited palette of narrative and artistic sources to fashion a particular perspective of decline in respect to the Roman Empire. For Sereni, the key engine of decline had been planted prior to the invasions, which he suggested caused "pillage, devastation and the inexorable decline of the old centres of urban life."[3]

3 Emilio Sereni, *History of the Italian Agricultural Landscape* (Princeton University Press, 1997), 47.

These tumultuous events were aided by economic decline and the "deep social divisions" of the Roman Empire. Whilst there is some truth in these characterizations, the realities they suggest simply will no longer do. In a study from 2007, the late Riccardo Francovich pinpointed the decline of production in Tuscany because of two factors: first, demographic reduction; and second, the concentration of population in a few villages, prompting the collapse of the Roman settlement pattern. This was reflected by a reduction in total sites from over two and a half thousand sites up to the fourth century, to a total of 201 sites from the sixth to the seventh centuries.[4] This is, of course, only a snapshot of Tuscany and would not have been meaningful throughout all of Italy. Continuities and shifts in priorities may sideline straightforward notions of decline in the landscapes. Even so, once the downward pressure on population levels eased with the cessation of regular plague events, economic activity begins to turn around its significant decline. It is likely that such improvement was localized and fragmentary, and certainly very slow (if not glacial) at first. As we move towards the eighth century, however, multiple factors may have assisted in a noticeable productive increase, notably the climate and agricultural and technological advances.

In rural contexts, the strategic depth of agricultural and pastoral production is impressive. Staple crops such as wheat, vines, and olives were cultivated; horses, sheep, pigs, and cattle were reared as essential components of the economic mix. Woodlands provided chestnuts, timber, and charcoal but also both summer and winter pastures. Earlier conceptions that envisaged afforestation as an indication of the return of a "savage forest" linked ineluctably with barbarian hordes and decline has given way to a view that sees woodlands as

4 Riccardo Francovich, "The Hinterlands of Early Medieval Towns: The Transformation of the Countryside in Tuscany," in *Post-Roman Towns, Trade and Settlement in Europe and Byzantium*, ed. J. Henning (De Gruyter, 2007), 135–36.

zones of human management, where pigs and sheep could flourish in the wooded pastures.

In the *ER*, a clear sense of the agrarian pursuits of the Lombards is simply exemplified by the wide range of regulations. Included in titles of the *ER* we have those that regulate domesticated stags, birds, bees, falcons, cows in calf, mares in foal, the tails of horses, and on chestnut, hazelnut, pear, and apple trees. Both boundaries and the protection of trees form a significant set of titles. Entering a courtyard in anger (*ER* no. 277) and trespassing into a garden to steal (*ER* no. 284) attracted penalties of twenty and six *solidi* respectively (Drew, 108–9). However, for the unfree being found in someone else's courtyard put them at risk of immediate death or, should they surrender directly, a fine of forty *solidi*, payable by their lord (Drew, 58–59). Six separate titles deal with protection of marked trees, penalizing those that add new marks of purported ownership. A freeman would be liable to a fine of eighty *solidi* for cutting down a marked tree or forty if a false mark is added. The penalty for a slave is again death for the former and the loss of a hand for the latter (Drew, 100). Woods were clearly important, as *ER* no. 302, which deals with olive trees, suggests. It fines individuals three *solidi* if they destroyed or felled an olive tree (in comparable terms, the composition for cutting off a slave's second finger was also three *solidi*). Finally, the profit to be had from woodland is suggested by a comment in *ER* no. 319, which deals with the extraction of honey. Should an individual find bees and their honey upon an unmarked tree, "they may take the honey" according to the "law of nature."

Riverine management was also dynamic and significant. At the heart of the Lombard Kingdom, the Po River and its tributaries held particular importance. The river, stretching from the Adriatic to its *Piemontese* origin, runs for nearly seven hundred kilometres, passing down through the cities of Turin, Piacenza, Cremona, and Ferrara (to name but a few). As the research of Sauro Gelichi has demonstrated, Comacchio was a significant entrepot at the end of this riverine system linking Byzantine and Lombard nautical networks. The Po itself has changed its course frequently, especially the estuary zone adjacent to the Adriatic Sea. We have evidence of its crucial importance for the Lombard Kingdom in the eighth century. A lost diploma of Liutprand agreed to supply the monastery of Bobbo with salted fish on payment of ten *solidi* a year from his estate of Garda. This distance is an impressive 160 kilometres. One can imagine the river as a key conduit for trade and connection between rural production zones. The *Pactum* agreed, again, between Liutprand and Comacchio—a rather dry list of river tolls and mooring dues—highlights trade in garum, pepper, and oil and also the interconnectivities across regions and the growing prevalence of transregional trade. However cogent a picture one may paint for the rural economies of Lombard Italy, as we have seen, close specificity of conditions in Tuscany cannot be extrapolated as a general model for either all geographical or chronological horizons of the Kingdom and, later, the entities in the south.

In the south, from 774 onwards, one may detect similar themes. Of course, there are evident problems with attempting a characterization of rural life across three centuries. There is some evidence of depopulation in the ninth century from narrative sources, featuring rather inflated figures, for instance, of individuals enslaved and on their way to Egypt; there are also rather more credible charter references to devastation of estates caused by war. Even if these do not permit secure extrapolations, it is safe to say that endemic war, raids, and destruction, particularly in the ninth century across the south, had a deleterious impact. This can be balanced against the revenues and benefits provided by transregional trade, although the relevant entrepots in the south (i.e., Naples, Amalfi, and Gaeta) were beyond Lombard political control for most of the period under discussion. Though we must consider variance in a local context, documents reveal the dynamic management of resources which may have been the key connection across the Lombard north and south. We see a similar impulse with urban and semi-urban communities.

Towns

Whilst the urban nature of Lombard elites has often been accepted, their contribution to cities has been relegated to that of "squatters" in a post-Roman world. Certainly, one does not need to search very far in the literature to find assertions of their "primitive" interventions into urban sites. Bryan Ward-Perkins in his description of urbanism in Early Medieval Italy as part of Ausenda's *The Langobards Before the Frankish Conquest* suggested that between the poles of "sunny optimism" (that towns had essentially weathered the storms of the sixth century in particular) and "apocalyptic pessimism" was "moderate gloom," the new consensus. There was, however, an important caveat that in comparison to "elsewhere," the scenario in Italy was better. Certainly, one may adduce a basic continuity in the physical organization of cities, where almost perfect Roman grid street patterns survived into the Middle Ages, but, as we shall see below and in a similar way to rural spaces, there are indications of both responses in the evidence. Until recently, a holistic analysis of the urban economic contribution had been undervalued. Caroline Goodson's *Cultivating the City* employed a sensitive set of evidential bases to discuss rural and urban landscapes in a nuanced picture of the quotidian realities in Lombard Italy. It is possible to ditch a black and white dichotomy where pre-Lombard Italy was inherently superior, where (to use the term favoured by older scholarship) towns underwent a "ruralization" process. The picture was clearly more complicated, and indeed a "hard" division between rural and urban in this period should be eschewed. It should also be cautioned that what "we" might consider or define as urban is not congruent with the early medieval reality. Were we to experience the lived reality of early medieval cities, we would find them limited in both overall population levels and physical extent.

Towns in Lombard Italy were sites of three interconnected activities which spiralled and linked into each other. First, they were places of institutional power where kings, dukes, and *gastalds* operated, called councils, and determined legal disputes; second, they were centres of episcopal and ecclesiastical power; and third, they operated as economic centres and links between regions and their productive lands. In institutional terms, Lombard elite networks were associated with cities and their immediate surroundings. In the earliest period of Lombard settlement, these centres were where the local dukes operated and controlled their territories. Between 574 and 584, when the Lombards had no kings, Paul the Deacon tells us that there were thirty-five cities which acted as the seats of power of the dukes (although he may have had his own eighth century in mind). He singled out for comment, *Ticinum* (Pavia), Bergamo, Brescia, Trent(o), and *Forum Iulii* (modern Cividale di Friuli). We might add to this list Verona, Monza, Milan, Asti, Lucca, Benevento, and Spoleto as centres of Lombard settlement and power in the first century of Lombard rule in Italy. In the Lombard South, Spoleto, Benevento, later Salerno, Bari, and Capua assumed institutional and political significance. Later, in the seventh and eighth centuries some cities had dukes, *gastalds*, and bishops who all held powers over the local elites. Lucca, the most useful example from the early eighth century, had a *dux* (Waltpert) and a bishop (Wal(t)prand) from the same family. Cities were used by elites to display their power and as centres of client networks. At the highest elite level, Lombard kings demonstrated their authority in Pavia, Milan, Monza, and Verona. In Milan in 604, for instance, Agilulf (590–616) used the amphitheatre as a venue for the formal elevation of his son, Adaloald, as co-ruler, which was witnessed by Frankish ambassadors. Over the course of the seventh century, however, Pavia assumed an increasing importance as the prime *sedes regiae* of the Kingdom. It was here that the principal political theatre of the Kingdom played out. Rothari and his successors promulgated new law, held consultations to make new law, and embellished the city as indications of their supremacy. Just two examples of this, noted from the *Historia Langobardorum*, are emblematic. Perctarit (661–662 and 671–688) built with "wonderful workmanship" a new gate in Pavia which adjoined the palace, and his wife, Rodelinda, built a new church called Holy Mother of God "At the Poles," which was adorned with "marvellous decorations" (*HL* 5.34, 1.36). Such foundations in cities also show the importance of ecclesiastical functions. In his *From Classical Antiquity to the Middle Ages: Urban Public Buildings in Northern and Central Italy*, Ward Perkins lists seven royal foundations in Pavia, four churches by episcopal patronage, and four endowments by secular or clerical aristocracy in the Lombard period. Most notable here was the foundation of *San Savino* by Peter (712–744), the bishop of Pavia, and the creation of a female monastery by Senator in 714. Away from Pavia, perhaps the picture is most evocative when we consider the evidence for church building in Lucca, which has the richest documentary footprint of the Kingdom. Here evidence from extant private charters reveals that no less than thirteen churches, *xenodochia*, and monasteries were endowed from shortly before 668 up to 775. Beyond the major centres noted above, smaller sites such as Cividale and Brescia retained importance courtesy of their links to Lombard elites that were tied to the dukes resident in these cities. Overall, this confluence of episcopal and ecclesiastical foundations in concert with royal and ducal activity provided a clear *raison d'être* for urban sites, but it was their economic functions that sustained them.

The economic aspect of towns and cities has attracted much attention in recent years, with it often being used as a yardstick to calibrate the health of the early medieval economy. Rather than a picture of unremitting decay and ruin, one may envisage urban sites as centres of production in gardens, orchards, and smallholdings within or adjacent to the towns. Towns were not just sterile sites where political and ecclesiastical powers operated. However, the situation varies across time and space. Ross Balzaretti makes the important point that as transregional and long-distance trade contacts shrivelled in the fifth and sixth centuries, the immediate hinterlands of cities, such as Milan, acquired a greater importance. Local economies developed their own solutions to demand pressures; village elites were linked into the networks of major landowners, be they secular or ecclesiastical, to supply cities with basic goods. We have already seen that riverine trade continued down the Po River from entrepots such as Comacchio and the Venetian lagoon into the Po plain heartland of the Kingdom. On the one hand, anecdotal evidence of the vitality of cities comes from a variety of materials. For Milan, we have the eighth century *Versum de Mediolano civitate*, which describes the city as "the queen of cities and mother of this country / rightly called by the name metropolis / Praised by the nations of all ages."[5] Verona in a later poem, probably modelled on the Milan item, was itself described as a city with "forty-eight towers in a circuit brilliantly gleam / and eight lofty ones among them are taller than all the others... / its streets are wondrously laid with flagstones."[6] As a ducal centre, Cividale in Friuli represents a more modest but, in Lombard terms, probably more representative centre for the Kingdom. A combination of archaeological data, extant architecture, and the rich plethora of notices furnished by Paul the Deacon would allow us to picture the city as a busy living and working centre in which the local elite were associated with the dukes. This is most clearly set out in Paul the Deacon's remarks on Pemmo of Friuli and his entourage in the early eighth century. On the other hand, not all urban sites survived the challenges of the fifth and sixth centuries. Two examples will suffice here. Aquileia, the subject of a lament probably written by Paulinus of Aquileia, never recovered from the attentions of the Huns. It was described as follows: "once you raised your head high in pride, now you lie shunned, useless / crushed and in ruins, never to be repaired for all time."[7] On the other side of the peninsula, Luni on the Ligurian coast, conquered by Rothari in the 640s, never seemed to recover from his direction that the Byzantine port cities be reduced to villages. One should, however,

---

5 Balzaretti, *The Lands of St Ambrose*, 139.

6 Christie, *From Constantine to Charlemagne*, 183–84.

7 Peter Godman, *Poetry of the Carolingian Renaissance* (Duckworth, 1985), 111.

be conscious that both environmental degradation and even economic impoverishment had already worked their magic on the site prior to Rothari's appearance.

Just as we have emphasized in respect of rural spaces, the tapestry of urbanism in Lombard Italy was deeply affected not only by local conditions and responses to specific events but also by longer-term factors that promoted or inhibited resilience and growth. As a final point, in a way, we only have glimpses, fragments of the organic realities of urban environments in the early medieval Italian landscape, but these are sufficient to give the impression that urban landscapes in Lombard Italy were evolving and dynamic places.

Chapter 2

Belief and Identities

Having considered the physical and functional worlds of the Lombards and the tangible footprints of rural space, towns, and trade, it is now imperative to consider the intangible, conceptual universe that the Lombards crafted and lived within. First, we shall consider the religious worlds of the Lombards; second, the constitutive elements of Lombard identities, how men and women fitted into the Lombard conceptual space; and finally, our discussion shall conclude with an analysis of law, knowledge, and learning in Lombard Italy, in many respects at the vanguard of the so-called Carolingian Renaissance of the late eighth and early ninth centuries.

Belief

In the museum attached to the Cathedral of Monza, one can still view the beautiful, gilded sculpture of a hen and her chicks bestowed upon Theodelinda—the resilient Lombard queen and wife of two Lombard kings—by Pope Gregory the Great in the sixth century (see Figure 3). This gift marks a pivotal moment in the religious history of the Lombards, which has proven to be such a perplexing issue for historians over generations. Religious loyalties mattered in the Early Middle Ages in a way that is often difficult to entirely comprehend in our own times. Characterized as the anarchists of the *Völkerwanderung* by Thomas Hodgkin, it seemed obvious at one time to associate their fearful military reputation with

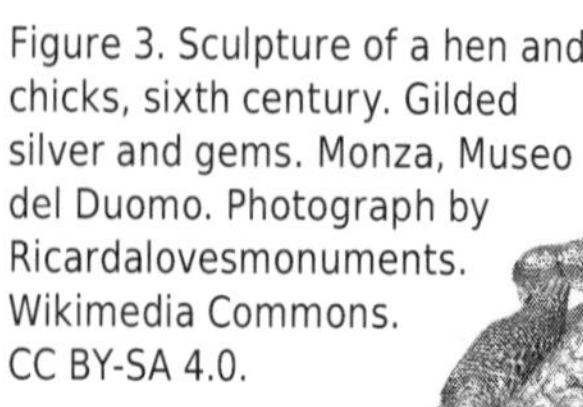

Figure 3. Sculpture of a hen and chicks, sixth century. Gilded silver and gems. Monza, Museo del Duomo. Photograph by Ricardalovesmonuments. Wikimedia Commons. CC BY-SA 4.0.

a stubborn and persistent paganism. The problem then and now is that such paganism is rather difficult, if not impossible, to demonstrate from credible written sources. Such sources that we do possess on the subject, such as the works and letters of Gregory the Great, are enshrouded in eschatological gloom and were coloured by Gregory's perceptions of the end of times. In picking up the issue, we need to commence with the references provided by Prokopios in his voluminous works on the wars of Justinian. We enter a complex world of alliance and counter-alliance manipulated, or at least contrived, by the machinations of the court in Constantinople, whose ostensible objective was to confound its neighbours to the north. Thus, Prokopios reports the efforts of the Lombards and the Gepids to acquire Imperial support.

In their delegation the Lombards are said to have reminded the emperor that they are catholic and orthodox and the Gepids are not.[1] Depending upon these references

1 Lower case "catholic" in this instance equates to those who adhered to the doctrines of the Church as set out by the universal councils. Thus, the use of "catholic" and "orthodox" before 1054

alone, however, would be injudicious. Roughly thirty years later, when the Lombards enter Italy, it is more than likely that there were pagans, "Arians," and catholics, all part of the religious mix that constituted the new arrivals in the peninsula. The Three Chapters Schism further added to the heterogeneous mixture of affiliation and doctrine which crossed over from Imperial to Lombard sides. Whilst Marta Szada in her *Conversion and the Contest of Creeds in Early Medieval Christianity* has recently reminded us of the contest of creeds on the ground, it would be problematic to see individual approaches to religious belief as static and immobile. Indeed, it is more likely that elements of salient beliefs rubbed shoulders with orthodox and non-orthodox approaches on the ground in a fashion that no doubt aggravated those entirely committed to one strand of belief above others. On the elite level of analysis which has preoccupied commentators due to an evident visibility, doubts and uncertainties still persist. Two issues are particularly important. First, the existence and persistence of paganism amongst the Lombards; and second, the level of commitment they may have had to Homoianism/"Arianism" in the first century of Lombard residence in Italy. We shall consider this first before we track forwards to set out how the Lombards could become, from their perspective, a catholic Christian Lombard nation and retain their orthodox credentials from 774 and beyond.

Pagans, Arians, and Catholics, 568–672

Earlier scholarship, no doubt influenced by the purple prose of Gregory the Great, portrayed the Lombards as incorrigible pagans who delighted in mindless vandalism and took no account of religious, let alone Christian, sensibilities. The reality on the ground, however, was fundamentally more

operates for all segments of the Church which acknowledged the decisions of the Council of Chalcedon in 451 and previous councils. It also implies acceptance of the Christological decisions made by those councils and the overall primacy of Rome.

complicated and indeed more interesting than this perception would suggest. It is a contentious issue to ascertain with any certainty whether the Lombards entered Italy as pagan or Christian, and if Christian, catholic or not. Indeed, this doubt has caused one eminent commentator to opine that the Lombards were not that interested in religion at all. Certainly, the evidence can be read that way, and when one undertakes a comparative view of the approach in the various so-called successor kingdoms, such as either Visigothic Iberia or Merovingian Gaul, one might conclude that there is a definite absence of engagement with religion. Yet, in some respects the sources we possess have misled historians and prompted a view which is unlikely to be congruent with the responses of individuals in the Early Middle Ages. Let us, first, consider the religious landscape that the Lombards encountered on their arrival into Italy.

Most commentators have assumed that by the second half of the sixth century Italy was essentially Christianized. This is not necessarily the case, although evidence to the contrary is rather difficult to find. The *Passion of Vigilius of Trent* (ca. 385–400/405) (probably written as late as the eighth century) does set out a story of a bishop who, in attempting to evangelize the "deep country" in the vicinity of Verona, Trent(o), and Brescia was killed by a "crowd of rustics" for "striking down" an "idol." The mob became enraged when Vigilius started to preach, having broken the "idol" and "swollen by diabolical inflammation [they] smashed in his holy head." This part of the Veneto/Trentino Alto-Adige is not so far off the beaten track that one might expect the ongoing processes of Christianization to have entirely missed out the region. It does, however, give us sufficient cause to pause and think about assumptions of the success of Christianity after the declaration of religious tolerance in 313. Of course, one should also be careful to distinguish the form of Christianity involved. In the north of Italy in the period, one might identify three strands of belief, not congruent with each other. First, the orthodox catholicism which looked to Rome for inspiration; second, the "schismatic" Tricapitoline bishops and their congregations who rejected the condemnation of the Three Chapters which were geographically concentrated in the north of the peninsula (and generally, but not exclusively associated with Lombard areas); and third, those who espoused an Arian/Homoian theology in direct opposition to the Chalcedonian tendencies of the first two groups. It was then a complex picture, often made more difficult to delineate due to the vicissitudes of geopolitics and the interventions of Constantinople.

The original appearance of the Lombards is not noted in the *Liber Pontificalis* (hereafter *LP*) and unusually they are not prime protagonists in pertinent hagiography of this period. The *Passion of Cetheus*, a hagiographical *vita* which includes a rare appearance of Lombards, is at least indicative of the variance and confusion of Italy in the late sixth century. In this story of the martyrdom of Cetheus of (modern day) Pescara we encounter two Lombard military commanders: Alahis and Umblo. As Nicholas Everett, the editor of an English translation, indicated, this item seems to have had a contemporary source behind its composition, which when reconciled with recent archaeological work in Pescara validates the broad contexts of the story set out. Even so, the hyperbole in the *vita* with reference to the Lombards makes the textual presentation a little difficult to accept at face value. Alahis and Umblo, depicted as the Lombard villains in the *vita*, are variously described as the "most evil and dishonourable men of this people, certainly the sons of concubines," the "most evil Umblo," or even the most "wicked" Umblo. The kernel of the story, however, pivots around the unstable division of the city between western and eastern parts held by each of the two Lombard leaders. In the subsequent conflict between the commanders Alahis is defeated and Umblo orders his execution. Meanwhile, Cetheus attempts to intervene, but he was, in turn, bound and killed. Missing in all of this is any suggestion of religious antipathy. The Lombards are simply associated with "inflicting barbaric destruction." In a similar fashion, in a notice in the *Historia Langobardorum*, and quite close to Pescara and to this period, Paul the Deacon notes an encounter between Ariulf, *dux* of Spoleto (592–602), and Sabinus (or Savinus) of Spoleto (d. 303), the martyred bishop of the Spoletan capital. According to Paul's story, Ariulf had seen a man fighting on his behalf against the Romans at Camerino, whom none of his men had noticed. Later, when Ariulf had come near to Spoleto, he entered the church of Savinus and realized that the "painted figure" within was the man who had protected him. Whilst Ariulf is described by Paul (*HL* 4.16) as "up this time...a heathen" (*gentilis*), he does not tell us directly that this prompted any change in Ariulf's religious loyalties, but neither does he make any comment on the general perspective of the Lombards who fought with the *dux*. A final example from nearly twenty years earlier is also worth considering. This was when the Lombard army encountered Hospitius of Nice (d. 581) in Provence. The Lombards, seeing Hospitius bound and dishevelled, thought that he was a murderer and tried to kill him, at which point the attacker was himself immobilized until Hospitius intervened. This Lombard, Paul tells us, "converted to the faith of Christ." Consequently, those who had listened to the words of Hospitius with care returned home safely, but those who despised his words "perished miserably" (*HL* 3.2). None of these anecdotal episodes is definitive in revealing the comprehensive religious impulses of the Lombards in the first years of their time in Italy, but they do at least confirm the plausibility of their paganism or even the mixed loyalties they held. We read in the *Dialogues* of Gregory the Great, for instance, that the Lombards are pagans "sacrificing the head of a goat to the Devil," and discover that one of the Lombard bishops was "of course an Arian."[2] Beyond the reports of elite encounters in narratives, however, one may attempt to balance the picture with the available evidence of burial patterns and the deposition of grave goods, although one must be careful not to simply equate grave goods with religious credence alone.

2 Odo John Zimmerman, *St. Gregory the Great: Dialogues* (Catholic University of America Press, 1959), 161–62, 163.

Neil Christie in his discussion of these issues in *The Lombards: The Ancient Longobards* pinpointed that there was a "striking" reduction in the provision of grave goods after 650. Whilst he was right to indicate that other factors may have come into view, one does wonder how the "Longobard open-mindedness" he suggests permitted a "progressive intake of Catholicism" could be effectively calibrated.

The letters of Gregory the Great reveal his "fear of the barbarity" of the Lombards, but at the same time he could correspond with both Agilulf and Theodolinda, the rulers of the Lombards, to encourage them to agree to and keep a peace with the Byzantine Empire. Paul the Deacon even transcribes two of these letters into the *HL*. Theodolinda, observes Gregory, holds the "true faith" whereas the pope praises Agilulf for his "prudence and goodness...[who]... in loving peace" shows that he also loves "God who is its author" (*HL* 4.9). There is no hint here that Agilulf and Theodolinda were neither catholic nor orthodox, or that the elite networks that worked around the Lombard kings were Arians/Homoians. The equivocal evidence—glimpses here and there—have permitted the construction of remarkable theoretical edifices, which project factional strife around religious allegiances (in other words, catholic vs. Arian). There is not space here to consider all aspects of this fascinating set of issues. That said, Gregory in writing to all the bishops of Italy in January 591 reported that the "most wicked [king] Authari (584–90)" had "prohibited the children of the Lombards from being baptized into the Catholic faith."[3] In view of the "grim pestilence," however, Gregory counselled his bishops to advise the Lombards to "reconcile" their children to the catholic faith. The question, then, is not whether there were Arians amongst the Lombards, but their quantity and their significance. Here the anecdotal notices of Paul the Deacon may be more of a hindrance than a help. He notes

3 *The Letters of Gregory the Great (Books 1–4)*, ed. John R. C. Martin (PIMS, 2004), 131–32.

that Rothari was Arian and (perhaps implausibly) suggests that each Lombard city had two bishops: one Arian and one catholic. Less familiar is a report from the *Life of Columbanus* by Jonas of Bobbio (*fl.* ca. 600–660), which described the contacts between Arioald (626–636) as both *dux* of Turin and king of the Lombards with the monastery.[4] Arioald declined to intervene in a dispute between Bobbio and Bishop Probus of Tortona, nor when king would he greet a certain Blidulf, one of those in the entourage of Abbot Athala, for he suffered from the "Arian disease" as Jonas names it.

Intertwined with the conundrum of Lombard Arianism is the progress of the Three Chapters Schism in northern Italy. Following the condemnations issued by the Council of Constantinople in 553, the churches of the north of Italy refused to accede to the anathemas promulgated. They collectively disapproved of papal support and were therefore technically schismatic. Efforts by Smaragdus, Exarch of Ravenna to resolve the schism by force were counterproductive. In any case, those bishops under the Lombard kings were able to avoid any physical compulsion, and the schism rumbled on throughout the seventh century.

Catholics and Arians, 672–774

Perctarit's second tenure as king does not, on the face of the sources we possess, signal a dramatic change from the approaches of his predecessors. Yet there are some intriguing clues which suggest that the king had set in motion several significant changes. These approaches are subsequently crystallized by the Synod of Pavia in 698 where the Three Chapters Schism between the northern Italian sees and the Papacy was finally put to bed. Liutprand's contribution, as we shall see below when we consider his law promulgation, is also significant, as it represents the culmination of a Lombard

4 *Jonas of Bobbio: Life of Columbanus, Life of John of Réomé and Life of Vedast*, ed. Alexander O'Hara and Ian Wood (Liverpool University Press, 2017), 229–30, 232–34.

orthodoxy confidently self-confessed. The *Carmen de synodo Ticinensi*, a poem in nineteen stanzas, reports the end of the Three Chapters Schism. This is also the only reference to the formal abolition of Arianism, which is attributed to the father of Perctarit, Aripert I (652–661). Perctarit, as the son of Aripert, is "credited" (*exempla patris*; presumably an attempt to emulate his *pius et catholicus* father) with baptizing the Jews. "Those who refused (baptism) were killed by the sword," indicates the poem. It continues to name Perctarit as a lover (*amator*) of the church and a *constructor* of monasteries. This last, at least, can be triangulated with notices in the *HL*, where Paul the Deacon reports (*HL* 5.33–34) that he built a convent in Pavia for "many virgins," and that he was a "pious man, a Catholic in belief." This is rather thin gruel for a significant set of changes, which sees the end of Arianism amongst the Lombards. Digging deeper, however, as Marta Szada has recently done, one may identify Arian texts that were erased in the seventh century, signifying not only a change in ownership but an inflective moment when Lombard Italy adopted a catholic and orthodox idiom.

We shall see below, when Lombard law is discussed, the Christocentric expression in the laws of Liutprand. On the ground, however, tangible elements of this new, vigorous orthodoxy were evident. Both the quixotic, Aripert II (701–712) and Liutprand returned the Cottian Alpine patrimony to the Papacy. Whilst one might take issue with the author of a marginal note that describes Aripert as *vera iustitia et sincera*, there is a greater range of evidence to consider with Liutprand.[5] At the very commencement of his rule, Liutprand made legal provision, for the first time, which permitted the Lombards to make testamentary donations to the Church "on behalf of his soul or to dispose of his property in whatever manner...is pleasing to him" (Drew, 146). Thus, Liutprand paved the way for a deepening of monastic foundation and donation to the church more broadly. Liutprand's own

5 Everett, *Literacy in Lombard Italy*, 288.

foundations included the remarkable church and monastery of St. Anastasius, which was attached to his rural suburban manor in Corteolona. Here Liutprand was able to compare his own catholicism in distinction to his contemporary, the Byzantine Emperor Leo III (717–741), who was instrumental in the Italian foment caused by his iconoclastic impulses. Both extant epigraphic testimony and Liutprand's involvement with the movement of the bones of St. Augustine from Cagliari to Pavia hint at more than just a sharp eye for propaganda; indeed, they amply demonstrate his personal piety expressed in the prologues to his laws.[6]

This official orthodoxy remained the key element in late Lombard kingship from this point onwards. Both Ratchis and Aistulf, who also issued amendments to the Edict, vaunted their catholic credentials. Aistulf, for instance, described himself in his prologue as "the most excellent king of the Catholic Lombard nation." Aistulf, decried by the *LP*, was behind the foundation of the monastery at Nonantola. The final Lombard king, Desiderius (757–774) and his wife, Ansa (†after 774), founded and embellished the monastery of San Salvatore in Brescia, when Desiderius was still *dux* of that city. His daughter, Anselperga, became the monastery's first Abbess. Despite this expression of catholicity, the Lombard kings of the eighth century all encountered determined antipathy on the part of the Papacy. Set out simply, this translated into active opposition to the hegemonic ambitions of Pavia. Liutprand acknowledged the moral authority of the popes in his law (see Title 33 from 723); as implicitly the kings that followed. Attempts by Desiderius to indirectly orchestrate Lombard control of Rome foundered in the factional circus operative in that city; and ultimately propelled the Frankish interventions that culminated in the end of the Kingdom.

6 Christopher Heath, *The Age of Liutprand: Dynamics of Power in Eighth Century Italy* (Bloomsbury, 2025), 81–88.

A Catholic Christian Lombard Nation, 774 and After

We have seen above that, progressively, one may detect a fusion of religious credence and political expression that forms an important part of the moral authority of kings from Perctarit onwards. The latter is transferred to Arechis II in Benevento from the end of the Kingdom. It was most tangibly shown by the links of the Beneventan princes with the monasteries of Montecassino and San Vincenzo al Volturno (to name but two). The activities of Arechis II are especially significant. Not only did he endeavour to craft a revitalized Lombard identity in the south (in a similar vein to Liutprand), but he also patronized the creation of new religious centres in Benevento and Salerno, to which he moved in the 770s. The palace church of Santa Sofia in Benevento itself was intended to emulate (albeit on a much smaller scale) Haghia Sofia in Constantinople. Beyond Benevento itself, the great monastic centres of Montecassino and San Vincenzo al Volturno not only marked the piety and patronage of the Lombard princes of the south but also acted (as we shall see in the section on Knowledge) as beacons of culture and Christianity in the south.

Christianity in the Lombard south had weathered the challenges of depopulation and invasion in the sixth century. Akin to the Kingdom in the north, the actual conversion of the Beneventan dukes is hard to discern. The much later (i.e., mid-ninth century) *Vita Barbati* describes Romuald I (671–687) as Christian but attached to obscure (not very convincing) pagan rituals and a golden statue of a viper. Barbatus, we are told, cut down the "abominable tree" that served as the site of pagan ritual and had the statue of the golden viper melted down, indicating that "those who served two lords could not be saved."[7] Even so, this depiction of Beneventan paganism seems to be more an artifice of the hagiographical author than a real reflection on the religious landscape in the south.

---

7 Everett, *Patron Saints of Early Medieval Italy*, 50–59.

By the turn of the eighth century, Beneventan rulers patronized and donated to Christian sites, including the important shrine of St Michael in Monte Gargano. Montecassino was re-established a second time ca. 718 by Petronax of Brescia, whereas San Vincenzo del Volturno was founded in 731, according to the *Chronicon Vulturnense*, by three noblemen from Benevento named Paldo, Tato, and Taso. In 744, Gisulf II's donation created the *Terra Sancti Benedicti*, the secular lands of the abbacy, which was a considerable block of territory. Cumulatively, all these monastic foundations, with their subsequent endowments, embodied the political and social strategies of rulers to enhance their own hegemony as social actors.

The precarious geopolitical positions in the south in the ninth century affected both Montecassino and San Vincenzo al Volturno. The latter was destroyed by Islamic raiders in 881 and the former was sacked in 883/4, when Abbot Bertharius was killed. The community of Montecassino moved away, first to Teano and then, from 914, to Capua, not returning to their original home until 949. The travails of the monks were eloquently set out by Erchempert of Montecasino in his *Historiola* in the late ninth century. In religious terms, Islamic protagonists formed a new significance throughout the south, clearly in competition with Christianity. It is difficult to identify how, for instance, organic Islam operated in Bari, although we are told that Sawdān, Amir of Bari, founded a congregational mosque in the city. Yet, despite the enfeeblement of the Lombard principalities in geopolitical terms, orthodox Christianity remained resilient and fused with Lombard identity.

In practical terms, cathedral churches tended to be small, and concomitantly bishops maintained limited powers in comparison to the great monasteries. The career of Bernard of Salerno (ca. 849–860), as Valerie Ramseyer identified, is illustrative here. In the *Chronicon Salernitanum*, he is portrayed as a pious man intent on prayer, relics, and the embellishment of his cathedral and other churches in Salerno, but he was not involved in the cut-and-thrust of political matters. One might make a case for the effective subordination of ecclesiastical appointments in this period to the Lombard princes, when, for instance, it was Gisulf II of Salerno who nominated Alfanus I as Archbishop of Salerno in 1058. Also, in the principality of Salerno in the early eleventh century the abbey of Cava dei Tirreni became both significant and powerful. Within eighty years, across the period when the Lombard principalities became increasingly attenuated, this Benedictine monastery accumulated over fifty dependent houses and an extensive landed patrimony.[8] The thread that binds the Beneventan duchy of the seventh and eighth centuries with the fluid landscape in the following three centuries was the close link between political and religious powers that continued to be expressed in catholic and orthodox idioms; this is a testament to the traditions initiated by Perctarit, Cunincpert (688–700), and Liutprand, and part of the constructed identity embodied in the Lombards of the *Mezzogiorno*.

Identities

There were several fault lines that ran within Lombard society. The most significant in terms of legal significance was that between men and women. Lombard law imagines a graded, hierarchical society whose members' significance is calibrated by their theoretical monetary value, as set out in some detail by the *ER*. These calibrations pivoted around the equally important division that operated between the free and the various formulations that equated to the unfree. The latter had a variety of distinctions that allow us to posit a continuum between the free and the unfree rather than a simple binary and absolute operation. Finally, one can distinguish variance between the Lombards and the indigenous Italo-Romans, who remained resident within and adjacent to Lombard Italy. First, let us look at men and women.

---

8 Valerie Ramseyer, *The Transformation of a Religious Landscape: Medieval Southern Italy 850–1150* (Cornell University Press, 2006), 159–60.

Women had no independent legal identity in Lombard law. This meant that their interests and their protection in law were enshrined in their close relatives and, where they had none, in the hands of the king or his agents. The individual who theoretically protected the woman was the *mundoald*, who was said to hold the *mundium* of the woman. All recensions of Lombard law carefully set out a plethora of possible scenarios that involved this legal guardianship, not least Liutprand's additions. It would not be correct, however, to see Liutprand's amendments as in any way an attempt to "liberalize" the regime or to provide legal independence to women generally. The impulse behind much of the law was the "proper" management and succession to property and land. In scenarios where a freeman had no sons to inherit, for instance, law went into some detail to delineate and ostensibly protect the interests of the female relatives in the absence of their independent legal status. In his first set of additions Liutprand set out the circumstances in which daughters could receive land and inheritance. First, he indicated that in the absence of legitimate sons, daughters could succeed as heirs; and second, both married and unmarried daughters should receive an equal portion of the inheritance; thirdly, should there be both sisters and daughters of the deceased, the title sets out a complicated contingent resolution. In legal terms, women were subordinated and their scope for independent action was circumscribed and limited. At the same time, however, both narrative and documentary materials reveal that women were not powerless social protagonists. Too much attention has revolved around the activities of elite women (for understandable reasons of evidence). One might adduce the apparent (but unlikely) power of Theodolinda to choose her second husband, after the death of Authari, and her role as co-ruler with her son Adaloald in the early seventh century. Adelperga's actions, after the death of her husband Arechis II in 787, might also suggest some room for women to manoeuvre in political contexts. These are, of course, not "ordinary" examples in terms of the broader condition of women in Lombard society.

More prosaic activity is demonstrated in scenarios where Lombard women undertook decisions about their lands and their lives. Certainly, one should be cautious in constructing a balance sheet that would purport to tip the balance in favour of women in this period. A document cited by Marios Costambeys does show, however, that families would and could make provision for their wives and daughters. In this bequest, a certain Teuderacius leaves the usufruct of several farms to his wife Ansa and one estate each to his daughters Teuderia and Rosa.[9] In Piacenza, in the first quarter of the eighth century, the famous charter of Anstruda (although not referenced as such at the time) records her "request" to provide her *mundium* to Sigirad and Arochis of Seprio, for three gold *solidi* and to permit her marriage to their *servus*. To take the charter at face value, however, would be a mistake, for it is evident that, in accordance with law, her father Autharenus consents to the arrangement, which may have secured Anstruda's personal status; in other words, despite marrying a *servus*, she was not enslaved herself. The matter is complex, as the recent discussion by Ross Balzaretti demonstrates, but at the very least it reveals the legal impotence of women in this period.

The various forms of unfreedom in Lombard society are set out in the Lombard laws. Scrutiny reveals that there are some anomalies and inconsistencies in the application of law dependent upon how unfree any given individual may have been. There were several categories of unfreedom set out in Lombard law. First, the *aldius/aldia*, which can be termed the "half-free," are equated with household slaves (*servi ministeriales*). The latter are defined as those who had been "taught, nourished and trained in the home" (Drew, 65). Herders, *servi rusticani* (field slaves), *bovulci* and ox or goatherders were all calibrated in a scale below the household slaves, with the goatherders at the bottom. The variance in terms of com-

9 Giorgio Ausenda et al. eds., *The Langobards Before the Frankish Conquest: An Ethnographic Perspective* (Boydell, 2009), 69.

position for murder, for instance, runs from sixty *solidi* for the *aldius/aldia*; fifty for the household slave; and only thirty for the *bovulci*, various herders, and the *servi rusticani*. One can see here, in terms of mathematical equality, that the half-free retains an elevated value. Elsewhere in the *ER*, one can identify further inconsistencies with how the *aldii* were dealt with. One title, *ER* no. 126, even links *aldii*, household slaves, and field slaves together when dealing with crippled limbs. On the other side of the continuum, later Lombard law from Liutprand seeks to differentiate the free into separate categories where the court official, or client of the king, the *gasindius* is valued at two hundred *solidi* (although this could be increased to three hundred); the *primus* three hundred; and the modest *exercitalis* one hundred and fifty (Drew, 170). These detailed values mirror the hierarchical principles applied in Lombard law, but one must wonder how absolutely they were applied at the time.

The final division we shall consider here is that between the autochthonous inhabitants of Italy and the Lombards. This issue and all the difficulties it embodies have exercised many commentators, not least Alessandro Manzoni, Gian-Piero Bognetti, Stefano Gasparri, and Paolo Delogu, to name but four across the last century or so. It was not necessarily the case that the unfree were simply all the Italo-Romans who lived under the aegis of the Lombards. The passage in Paul the Deacon's *HL* which deals with the subject of tax, tributary subjects, and, separately, the murder of Italo-Roman landowners is an eighth-century red-herring applied to conditions of the late sixth century. It will not do to assume that all Italo-Romans resident in Italy were reduced to a servile condition. References in narrative sources are relatively modest. Gregory of Tours mentions a "Paul" in reporting the arrival of messengers in Gaul, wherein he said that Authari was dead "and Paul had taken his place."[10] Were we to make

10 Lewis Thorpe, *Gregory of Tours: The History of the Franks* (Penguin, 1974), 551.

the risky assumption that this Paul was Roman, it would add further intrigue to the murky world of court politics in the late sixth century. Roughly a hundred years later, Paul the Deacon (*HL* 5.37) provides a notice about the lust of Cunincpert for "Theodote, a girl sprung from a very noble stock of Romans," whom he had encountered in the baths of Pavia. The noble Senator, son of Albinus, who founded a monastery in 714 is a further example of the survival of the Italo-Romans at the heart of the Lombard Kingdom. Analysis based on onomastics alone, of course, is problematic, but certainly by the eighth century one begins to see composite Lombard and Latin names such as Daviprand, Bonuald, and Nazirimda. There are also tantalizing references to Romans and Roman law in Lombard legal titles. The application of Roman law in the period post-568 may have meant that both codes operated in tension, but Liutprand's titles simply provide direction when Romans marry Lombard women, instruct scribes to cite Lombard or Roman law correctly, and adopt what is contained within their codes (Drew, 183, 199).

Ultimately, the fusion of Lombards and Italo-Romans may be envisaged to have completed its cycle by the eighth century. In Lombard Benevento, whilst the ruling elite network retained its Lombard identity, the population they ruled cannot be viewed as "Lombard" in origin but by acculturation. In the late ninth century, the new Byzantine theme of *Langobardia* retained an affinity with Lombard identity, which, as we shall see below, was attractive to the indigenous elite. Melo, who led the ill-fated rebellions against the Empire, was described as Langobard by birth, free but dressed in the Greek fashion with a turban.

Chapter 3

Law, Governance, and Knowledge

Law

As a normative yardstick of life in Lombard Italy, the Lombard laws are an invaluable treasure trove. Thomas Hodgkin, usually quite sober in his opinions, observed that the "Code of Rothari...[was] like the black tent of the Bedouin pitched amid the colonnades of some stately Syrian temple, whose ruined glories touch no responsive chord in the soul of the swart barbarian."[1] A more positive portrayal, without pejorative cultural assertions, however, is possible. Lombard law can reveal the responses and impulses of Lombard rulers to everyday problems. One may explore their attempts to resolve issues and to guide the inhabitants of the Kingdom within a societal framework designed to retain balance and equilibrium. The first written iteration of Lombard law was issued by Rothari in November 643 in his *ER*. Although Grimoald in 668 and Ratchis and Aistulf in the 750s all expanded and added to Lombard law, the most notable contribution was made by the nearly annual additions of Liutprand, who added a further 153 titles to the original 388 of the *Edictum* between 712 and 735. Finally, Arechis II (758–787) and Adelchis (853–878) of Benevento issued modest additions of their own. Obviously, there isn't space here to consider all aspects of the law at

1 Thomas Hodgkin, *Italy and her Invaders. Volume VI, Book VII: The Lombard Kingdom 600–744* (Clarendon, 1895), 238.

length, but some exploration of the intent, remit, and particular focus of the law will be useful, because it will allow us to engage with basic issues, such as the envisaged normative framework for society and how it was thought that problems could be solved.

To understand the conceptual foundations of Lombard law, we should start with the programmatic intent of the Lombard kings and rulers who crafted the law. The prologue to Rothari's *ER* is particularly evocative and important. It should be noted that by the time of enactment the Lombards had been resident in Italy for nearly eighty years. Akin to their settlement into Italy, they did not inherit a pristine situation where the Lombards could start afresh. Neither the Italo-Romans nor their Roman law ceased to exist with their arrival, and in areas of Lombard control one can envisage that both forms of law operated, and there may have been some tension in what, how, and upon whom which law would apply and how one would resolve inconsistencies and/or scenarios where individuals professed one or other legal system. Here is not the place to discuss the personality of law and how/if such principle applied in Lombard Italy, but Paul the Deacon supplies an interesting reference which may assist. As we shall see in the next chapter, the initial settlement of the Lombards into Italy was propelled by a heterogeneous group of peoples, including a contingent of Saxons. Soon after the death of Cleph (572–574), and within the *interregnum*, Paul reports that the Saxons "were unwilling to be subject to the commands of the Langobards," and crucially, so he tells us, "it was not permitted to them by the Langobards to live according to their own laws" (*HL* 3.6). Consequently, they elected to leave. Taking Paul at face value for events of the late sixth century, when he writes two centuries later, is of course somewhat problematic, but even so the response of the Langobards is a telling one. Rothari's later impulse to issue an overarching edict may reflect an attempt to remove uncertainties and tensions between operating forms of law. The Prologue hints at this very point, when he declared that "we have perceived it necessary to improve and to reaffirm the present law, amending all earlier laws by adding that which is lacking and eliminating that which is superfluous." There are, in addition, several striking remarks in this Prologue which are worth reference. The Prologue indicates, first, that it was issued with the "principal Judges" (*primatos iudices*); second, that the Lombards had been led to the land of Italy "by the divine providence" (*divina potentia*); and third, that the king's "care and solicitude" (*sollicitudinis cura*) for the welfare of his subjects recognized "the numerous demands of the wealthy which should carry weight, but also the burdensome trials of the poor are important" (Drew, 39).

The prologues in Liutprand's additions, over many years, are remarkable in themselves, but when compared to Rothari's law, they demonstrate the inflected change that Lombard society had experienced over the course of the seventh century. In the first set of additions from his first regnal year (i.e., in 713), Liutprand emphasized the collective nature of law enactment. As Rothari had, he references the judges but also indicates that they came from all the areas of the Lombard Kingdom, including Tuscany, and adds "as well as with the reminder of my sworn Lombard *fideles*, and with the rest of the people attending." Liutprand also elevates into the Prologue a Christocentric and catholic view of kingship and law creation. He is a "Catholic Christian prince" [who] has been "influenced to promulgate these laws and to judge wisely not by his own foresight but through the wisdom and inspiration of God." Asserting thereafter that "the heart of the king is in the hand of God," which had been "attested" by the "most wise Solomon," Liutprand also credited divine providence as his inspiration: "to delete and add those things...which seem fitting to us according to the law of God." Liutprand's subsequent prologues evidence an association between kingship, orthodoxy, and the catholicism of the "most happy and Catholic, favoured by God, nation of the Lombards." Running concurrently as a significant strand of concern, however, is a practical desire to address specific gaps in the laws and to resolve contingent difficulties not previously envisaged. Thus, in the Prologue to the laws of 734, Liutprand indicated that "it is now our concern to add to the body of our lawbook laws covering a few cases which have recently arisen and were found not to be covered in the Edict." Consequently, the judges "had found themselves in doubt when rendering a decision" (Drew, 144–45, 207).

This practical quality of Lombard law is evident in all iterations and additions that were enacted. Rothari's *ER* endeavoured to craft a comprehensive set of legal remedies to all aspects of life and governance, in modern terms covering criminal, family, civil, and contract law. Azzara and Gasparri's typology (which Nicholas Everett follows) is an effective method of division of the concerns addressed in the *ER*. The first section (the first thirteen titles) dealt with issues that affect what might be termed the public authority, whereas the second section covers injuries and offences against the individual. The second section has attracted considerable attention because it rehearses a carefully organized list of (often grotesque) injuries. The calibration sets out values of compensation commensurate with the legal status of the individual concerned; that is, according to rank (*in angargathungi*), as the title on murder described it. For example, a freeman who suffers the excision of his big toe could expect sixteen *solidi* in compensation; whereas an *aldius* (half-free) could anticipate four *solidi* as recompense; and a field slave merely two *solidi* to the slave's owner (see *ER* nos. 69, 96, and 120, respectively). Beyond these titles, there is law that concentrates on damage to property (nos. 146–52); succession (nos. 153–77); marriage law (nos. 178–223); and property ownership (nos. 227–44). This concentration on property and the rightful transmission of tangible assets is itself a revealing indicator of the structural concerns of Lombard law. In other words, these are the basic structures within which the king and his advisers envisaged local elite networks would operate. Titles 253 to 358—categorized as "minor crimes and damages"—are equally evocative of Lombard society as a rural one attempting to deal with a heterogeneous set of issues. Take, for instance, these three laws: no. 285 on fences; no. 286 on fence boards; and no. 287 on fence poles.

These titles redress physical boundary infractions. Whilst in general these are small matters, their presence in the *ER* demonstrates the contemporary and specific intent of the law to resolve problems before they escalated beyond control. Resolution in these clauses is by way of monetary compensation, as one would be expected to pay six *solidi* for breaking a fence (called *idertzon* in the text); stealing fence boards (*axegias*) attracted a fine of one *solidus*; and the fine for taking a fence pole was one *solidus*, but a cross pole incurred a fine of three *solidi*.

Whilst the *ER* attempted to be a comprehensive code, Rothari's successors took up the challenge they said he had made, as Grimoald's prologue of 668 suggested, "to add" to the "lawbook those provisions which we have been able to recover of particular causes which up to the present have not been recorded" and to "amend those provisions...that seem harsh and unjust." Whilst there are only nine additional titles in Grimoald's additions, Liutprand's legislative program is impressive, richly detailed, and compiled at least fifteen sets of additions across twenty-four years of his kingship. The distinctive Christianizing elements of his prologues have already been mentioned, but within the body of his law one sees several thematic strands which intertwine. One might be tempted to see here the crafting of a new moral regime which emplaces Christian approaches at the forefront of legal remedy. This is exemplified by the additions provided in his fifteenth year (i.e., 727) and neatly summarized by the Prologue from that year. In the first place, Liutprand reiterates the impulse that he adds laws "to the edict covering those matters for which judgement has been uncertain before this time inasmuch as some of our judges wish to conclude them according to custom, others according to their own discretion" (Drew, 180). Such enunciation demonstrates Liutprand's intent to regulate and control the capillary system of judicial governance, so discretion to decide doubtful matters falls to him in Pavia. Other titles explicitly set out the route by which appeals should reach the king but also circumscribe the competences for royal agents. Liutprand also elaborates on a new moral Christian regime for the Lombards by stating that "in defence of our Christian and Catholic law we make provision that no one may presume to wander from the faith of Christ, so that we may have God as a defender and helper firmly and permanently in all things" (Drew, 180). A comparison of this statement with the actions of Liutprand's predecessors, Rothari and Grimoald, reveals how far the entanglement of law creation and religious orthodoxy fundamentally re-energized Lombard kingship. When one considers further Liutprand's actual titles in this one year alone, one finds the fusion of these impulses in his law. On the one hand, title nos. 84 and 85 deal with "him who seeks the advice of a sorcerer" (*ariolus*) and "what is to be done if the judge or other public officials of a place fail to seek out sorcerers or witches"; whereas, on the other hand, title no. 86 deals with "what a man shall do if he finds someone else's horse doing damage to his property" and title no. 88 deals with "fugitive slaves" (Drew, 180–83).

The last set of additions issued by Liutprand was made in 735, a full nine years before his death. One may speculate as to the causes behind this lengthy gap, but once he had died and his nephew Hildeprand was replaced as king by Liutprand's client *dux*, Ratchis, we see a further set of additions issued by Ratchis in two sets. Another thirty-one titles were added by his brother, Aistulf. No further amendments were enacted by Desiderius, the final Lombard king. There are similar impulses behind the legislation of the two kings. Ratchis added fourteen titles to the lawbook, ostensibly, as the Prologue from the laws of 745 or 746 informs us "that all men, the powerful as well as the poor, who seek justice, may not be put off at all." The titles themselves exhibit both practical concerns and efforts to deal with the new realities of the mid-eighth century. What is striking here again, however, is the lengthy performative Prologue to the second set of additions of Ratchis. It provides a precis of law under his predecessors, in similar vein to the first legal titles of Liutprand from 713, but significantly refers also to the example of Liutprand, who is described as "that most glorious and orthodox supporter of the faith and ruler of this nation and...our instructor (i.e., *nutritor*), the exceptional and lofty Liutprand" (Drew, 218). In terms of actual law, his first title from 745 or 746 deals with the duties and responsibilities of his judges in the regions of the Kingdom beyond the court. Ratchis bemoans that he could not "go anywhere or attend any celebration or ride anywhere without being besieged by the appeals of many men" (Drew, 216). Such complaint might hint at dissonance in the capillary structure of judicial governance that Liutprand had so carefully adumbrated, but it also demonstrates that the local idiom of power upon which the Kingdom depended could be effectively "hijacked" by elite networks beyond Pavia. Ratchis admonished the judges to hold court every day and, in turn, to ensure that those directly under their control should also undertake their duties diligently and effectively. If any judge or local official failed to act, Ratchis indicated, "no patron will be able to intercede to prevent his losing that office" (Drew, 217). The subsequent law of Aistulf, who supplanted his brother as king in 756, was also composed of titles that updated previous law, dealt with new conditions, and determined what to do with unexpected and contingent matters. One example of this was title 15, which dealt with "those who throw dirty water on a wedding party." In line with previous approaches, Aistulf enjoined a considerable compensation payment (the enormous sum of nine hundred *solidi* if the offence was made by a freeman) so that neither a future *scandalum* or murder would occur as a result.

With the end of the Kingdom in 774, later Lombard law was created by two Beneventan princes. These are framed as continuations of the legal culture of the Kingdom, and in that sense alone are significant, but they have received less historiographical attention. Arechis II (758–787) added seventeen new titles, and Adelchis (853–878) added a further eight a century or so later. The laws of Arechis and Adelchis both attempt not only to "plug into" the inherited Lombard legal tradition, but also to mark a new iteration of Lombard identity in the south. Arechis, for instance, seeks to add explicit provision where none existed previously. In title no. 4 he indicated:

> The old jurists have avoided decree on several crimes, since they believed these could not occur, and have left errors to posterity. Since evil has been increasing, these crimes are now believed to be possible and...these deeds are visible, a thing which is wicked to say. And until now, because religious people are considered persons both unarmed and worthy of veneration in all respects, no law of composition established by a judicial reckoning has become evident concerning the homicide of religious people.[2]

The *capitula* of Adelchis are introduced by a remarkable prologue which provides a lengthy commentary on the Lombards' Kingdom in the north where the kings "happily ruled," Adelchis imitated his predecessor to eradicate the "wickedness of certain men," and he provided titles designed to update and reframe Lombard law so that it was congruent with ninth-century problems and perspectives. Whilst these last additions may have had limited local impact, the inheritance of Lombard law was to long outlast both the political and institutional structures of the Kingdom and to form part of the hybrid and vibrant legal cultures of the Italian *Duecento* and *Trecento*.

Governance

Whilst the law codes and their titles tell us a lot about the conceptual underpinning of any given society and how it was envisaged societies should work, they do not reveal how organic societies worked in practice. One of the analytical difficulties with Lombard law, particularly in the period of the Kingdom up to the early eighth century, is the absence of direct evidence for its application to specific circumstances. Some of the issues in this regard can at least be satisfied

2 Julie Anderson, "Historical Memory, Authority, and the Written Word: A Study of the Documentary and Literary Culture at the Early Medieval Court of Benevento, 700–900CE" (PhD diss., University of Toronto, 2017), 256.

with reference to narrative materials or from later charters.[3] Having already considered the patchwork of identities and the tensions between them in a Lombard context above, we need to explore how Lombard society operated both in the north before 774 and in the south subsequently.

The Lombards, we are told, when they left Pannonia behind took "their wives and children and all their goods." Within the year, the Lombards controlled large swathes of the north of Italy. At this point, in a passage much discussed, Alboin decided to entrust *Forum Iulii* to his nephew, Gisulf, who was his *marpahis*. Gisulf agreed, so long as Alboin would bestow upon him the "*faras*, that is the families or stocks of the Langobards that he himself wished to choose" (*HL* 2.9). The notice is an early indication of how Lombard society came to be organized. Power from the kings and Pavia was mediated to the dukes in the localities and the regions of the Kingdom. Throughout the duration of the Kingdom, this set of relationships, sometimes in tension but always at variance between kings and dukes, operated as the key dynamic. Amongst some of these dukes there was nearly complete independent scope for action, notably in Spoleto and Benevento. Those installed in Friuli are chronicled by Paul the Deacon, and here we see across the longer term, a freedom of action that was close to complete autonomy broken up by moments of closer supervision and scrutiny by the Lombard kings. Such independence of action, however, begins to shift as we enter the eighth century. Paul the Deacon reports in a lengthy notice how Liutprand removed Pemmo of Friuli and replaced him with his son Ratchis. This is emblematic of the renewed impetus for governance that Liutprand promoted. His legislation sets this out most clearly when he depicts a capillary system of rule, which runs from the humble *centenarii*, via the *schultheis*, to the *gastalds*, dukes, and ultimately to the kings in Pavia. Ratchis set this out clearly again in 745/6, when he directed that judges supervise their underlings appropriately

3 Everett, *Literacy in Lombard Italy*, 168.

on pain of both his office and wergild. This reiteration of the system might suggest that the organic functioning of this "system" was affected by realities on the ground. Interventions by the Lombard kings in the regions demonstrates that, no matter how powerful, they still had to negotiate with local power brokers. Even royal agents had to be encouraged to operate faithfully. Liutprand's *Notitia de actoribus regis* of 733 is illustrative of this, requiring royal officers to swear their fidelity to the king and to tell Pavia if matters seemed to be awry (Drew, 168–69).

Below the dukes in the regions, local networks linked and connected the powerful with the *gastalds* and the dukes. Client networks at this level were important, although clear glimpses of how they operated are relatively few and insufficient to safely extrapolate as universal in form and function. The (in)famous dispute between Siena and Arezzo regarding their ecclesiastical jurisdictions, at least, reveals the pressure the humble and the poor may have experienced when officers of the court investigated specific issues. This dispute also highlights the urban residence of aristocratic elites who seem to have held rather modest levels of property (when compared with contemporary elites elsewhere in western Europe). According to the definition supplied by Aistulf in his law, a noble was one who held at least seven properties (*casas massarias*). This is a relatively modest qualification to be a member of the elite in the Kingdom. Taido, a *cives* of Bergamo, for instance, whose will was made at the point when Pavia was besieged in 774, as a *gasindius* of the king (i.e., retainer) only possessed eight *curtes* in the areas of Bergamo, Sirmione, and Verona.

Once we consider the worlds of the free but modest landowners, or peasant farmers, we are not blessed with sufficient details to make generalizations that operate across all regions or periods in Lombard Italy. Perhaps best known, due to the survival of the documentation, from the very end of the Lombard period in the north, is the dossier of Toto (d. ca. 810), son of Arechis of Campione, who gave his land to the archbishop of Milan in 777. The family had been active from the 720s and managed several estates together with dependents. Toto continued to hold usufruct of the land after his donation, no doubt using his connection to the archbishop as a protective shield to his status and local prominence.

Knowledge

Looking back from the late eighth century, Paul the Deacon highlighted those who he believed had adorned the times of the Emperor Justinian (527–565) with their intellect and knowledge. He singled out for attention Cassiodorus (ca. 490–ca. 583) as knowledgeable in matters "human and divine," Dionysius (*Exiguus*) (ca. 470–ca. 544) for his calendrical computations, Priscian of Caesarea (*fl.* 500s) for his grammar, and finally Arator (ca. 490– after 544) as a "wonderful poet" (*HL* 1.25). The intellectual and cultural world that the Lombards inherited was one plugged into the Mediterranean *oikoumene*, with Constantinople at its centre. Their arrival, whilst unreported in the *LP*, had profound implications for the interconnections between the Kingdom and the wider Mediterranean world. That said, Lombard Italy should not be envisaged as a cultural *cul-de-sac*. At the end of the eighth century, for instance, the careers of several scholars at the court of Charlemagne evidence a flourishing intellectual climate in the Kingdom. The cumulative impacts of Paul the Deacon, Peter of Pisa (744–799), Paulinus of Aquileia (ca. 726–802/4), and others who were all part of the first wave of Charlemagne's collected scholars went far beyond the borders of Italy.

If we track back to the sixth century, however, Secundus of Non (d. 612?) was an Italian exemplar of the chronicle writing traditions of the west; his now lost work was used as a template by (perhaps) the composer of the *Continuation of Prosper* and by Paul the Deacon nearly two centuries later. His example, however, was not taken further in Lombard Italy. The work of Secundus fell within the period that Bognetti called the *estate dei morti* (summer of the dead) of Roman Italy. In other words, a last sparkle of Roman civilization and culture before fundamental cultural adjustments shifted Lombard Italy into a new idiom of expression. Thereafter, extant historical writing is limited to the *OgL*, which is significantly associated with the manuscripts of the *ER*. More broadly, however, using historical works as a yardstick of cultural and intellectual health will not work. Latinate ecclesiastical culture was sufficiently healthy to link the Late Antique worlds with the Carolingian "Renaissance." In the late seventh century, associated with the court in Pavia, we have evidence of a continuing tradition of learning. Whether or not the impetus or even the sustenance of this came from the monastery of Bobbio, founded earlier in the seventh century, is difficult to assert with evidential confidence, but even so Bobbio had a role to play in cultural outputs. Both Damian of Pavia (d. 711) and his deacon Thomas of Pavia were active in literary culture at the time of Aripert II and Liutprand. Paul the Deacon recalls a certain Felix "renowned in the grammatical art," and we should also mention a certain Stephanus, a *magister* who may have composed the *Carmen de synodo Ticinensi*.

The line of instruction passed from Felix to Flavian, the teacher of Paul the Deacon who, we may assume, Paul encountered at some point when resident in Pavia. Whilst it is then clear that Pavia was an important centre for learning, further depth to this picture may be added when we recollect that Paulinus of Aquileia, Peter of Pisa, Fardulf, and Paul himself were but four individuals all at the forefront of the program of Carolingian *correctio*, all with links and connections to Lombard aulic centres. As an intellectual and writer, Paul the Deacon's contributions are impressive for both their depth and range. His works include general histories (*HL*, *Historia Romana*), hagiography (*Vita Sancti Gregorii magni*), specific work tailored to patrons (*Gesta episcopum Mettensium*), poetry, and much more. Paul's historical scholarship taken alone had a profound, indelible impact on subsequent history-writing in Italy. Andrew of Bergamo's *History*, Erchempert of Montecassino's *Historiola* (both from the late ninth century), and the *Chronicon Salernitanum* (from the tenth century) all demonstrate a link back to Paul's work.

Figure 4. Detail of Lombard stonework, eighth century. Pavia, Musei Civici. Photograph by Fabio Romanoni. Wikimedia Commons. CC BY-SA 4.0.

In the south, the monasteries of Montecassino and San Vincenzo al Volturno acted as cultural beacons and pivots for networks of knowledge. Montecassino had been the final home of Paul the Deacon, and it is here that most scholars have assumed that he died. His pupil Hilderic is best known for his epitaph composed in honour of Paul. Yet, as Sven Meeder has shown in a recent contribution, the networks of intellectual connection threaded Montecassino into a Western European panorama.[4] Considering the contents and connections of specific manuscripts helps to form a rounded view but also demonstrates the intellectual preoccupations of the monastery which in turn fostered the activities of Hilderic and Erchempert in the two generations immediately after the demise of Paul the Deacon.

Beyond the monastery walls, however, the Beneventan duchy and its successor entities hosted a flourishing cultural world (Figure 4). Epigraphy in the south flowed from a robust tradition that operated in the Lombard Kingdom and includes exquisite examples such as the epitaphs to Cunincpert and to Bishop/Abbot Cumianus of Bobbio (ca. 641– ca. 736). In the

4 Sven Meeder, "Monte Cassino's Network of Knowledge: The Earliest Manuscript Evidence," in Elina Screen and Charles West, eds., *Writing the Early Medieval West: Studies in Honour of Rosamond McKitterick* (Cambridge University Press, 2018), 131–45.

south, this tradition continued, becoming a testament to the linked traditions between rulers and ruling families but also a method to communicate and project dynastic authority.

Julie Anderson highlighted the variance in what she called the "language of legitimacy" across the eighth and ninth centuries. At the head of this tradition we find, once again, Paul the Deacon, who may have composed inscriptions for the building projects of Arechis II. The son of Arechis, Grimoald III"s funerary inscription survives in the notice in the *Chronicon Salernitanum*, which highlights that "he was of royal ancestry from both parents/however, his lofty deeds exceed his birth / Powerful in lands, by far the most illustrious in arms/he was at this time the sure hope for the safety of the Samnites / Wondrous in appearance, but more extraordinary in his acts." Sico's epitaph also rehearses similar responses: "Here the body of the great Prince Sico rests, weep for him bitterly, O Benevento! / Sprung from a lineage of kings, he was more noble and powerful than his ancestors, such that none among them was equal or comparable [to him] / Mighty in figure, he was born in Ausonia after it was conquered by the slaughtering Franks."[5] This conscious evocation of knowledge and Lombard identities runs through subsequent aulic elite production and historical writing. Even later writers such as Radoald of Salerno and Amatus of Montecassino embodied a continuance of Italian historical writing in the ninth and tenth centuries, which continued through to the historians of Norman Sicily.

5 Anderson, *Historical Memory*, 60, 67.

Chapter 4

The Kingdom: Pavia, 568–774

The creation of the Lombard Kingdom in Italy was no straightforward, linear process. Yet by the time of Agilulf's death in 616 it had managed to weather the existential storms of the twenty years from 574 onwards, when its continuance stood in some doubt. The Kingdom was also able to craft out from the geopolitical chaos an enduring presence in the Italian peninsula, both north and south. Whilst this chapter is not intended to provide a detailed blow-by-blow account of the 206 years of the Kingdom's existence in the north, it will consider three broad periods of Lombard rule: first, the foundation and survival of the Kingdom which also saw the creation of autonomous Lombard entities based in Spoleto in the centre of Italy and Benevento in the southern uplands of the *Mezzogiorno*; second, a period that runs from Adaloald's (616–626) assumption of rule in 616 until the conclusion of a Lombard *Thronwirren* in 701 which had seen the Kingdom contested by a myriad of claimants; and third, the last and most powerful expression of the Kingdom when it had attained a hegemonic position in the peninsula until its conquest by Charlemagne (768–814) in 774 and the end of a Lombard idiom of power in northern Italy. We shall here consider the internal dynamics of the Kingdom, how it operated and how the rulers tackled the challenges of governance that inevitably arose between the centre and regional localities. Before we do this, however, we should return to that moment when Alboin first entered Italy.

Invention and Survival, 568–590

Writing over two hundred years later, Paul the Deacon contrasted the reaction of the Lombards to the alleged invitation of Narses, the Byzantine *generalissimo*, to cross into Italy. They received the "glad tidings which they themselves had also been desiring," he wrote, "and they formed high expectations of future advantages." Meanwhile, across from Pannonia in Italy, "terrible signs were continually seen at night... fiery swords appeared in heaven gleaming with that blood which was afterwards shed" (*HL* 2.5). This contrast fails to account for the realities on the ground in the Italian peninsula, which had endured a complex series of conflict, war, and violence which had gripped the peninsula from the advent of the Ostrogothic Wars from the 530s onwards.

Even though Paul the Deacon writes later, his narrative presentation retains considerable influence and value. His account of the arrival of the Lombards in Italy pauses at the point at which Alboin "ascended a mountain which stands forth in those places and from there as far as he could, he gazed upon a portion of Italy" (*HL* 2.8). Of course, we shall never know what Alboin was contemplating as he stood and looked across from his vantage point; nor, indeed, can we know what his intentions were as he returned to his composite army before leading them across the high pass into Friuli. With this journey we attain the culmination of Lombard migrations across many centuries, as they embark on their settlement in Italy where they will maintain a significant role in Mediterranean history for the next six centuries.

Once there, Paul the Deacon asserted that, "without any hindrance," Alboin and the Langobards entered the province of *Venetia* and propelled themselves westwards across the Po plain towards Milan and Pavia. If one were to read the *HL* carelessly, one might form the impression that the Langobards had it all their own way as they moved deeper into northern Italy. This would be a mistake. Recent analysis, notably by Sihong Lin and Eduardo Fabbro, has demonstrated how fluid, even chaotic the prevalent situation was at this time. This is in distinction to how most commentators had long viewed the twenty years from ca. 550. Previously, many historians viewed the Imperial conquest of Italy by the forces of Justinian to conclude with the capture of Verona in either 561 or 562, and that this signified the definitive end of Ostrogothic Italy. After this protracted effort, it was thought, the East Roman/Byzantine authorities were simply exhausted and incapable of offering any effective resistance against the new appearance of an armed group from the northeast. Thus, it was suggested that not only did the Lombards make rapid progress across the three years of Alboin's rule, but also that the resistance to him was meagre and ineffective. A careful review of all the available evidence should give us pause for thought about this seamless triumph.

There are several difficulties to consider. The first of these is the status and, thus, the rationale for the Lombards' arrival. We have already touched upon the alleged "invitation" received by the Lombards from Narses, who controlled the Byzantine military forces in Italy. Neil Christie and Francesco Borri have examined this issue in detail. Christie pondered in his article whether the Lombards had invaded or were invited. We might think that an invitation makes good sense when we recollect the context of Lombard and Imperial relations earlier in the 560s. When resident in Pannonia, the Lombards had been enmeshed into the nexus of imperial alliance and counter-alliance. They were allied with Constantinople against the adjacent Kingdom of the Gepids which Alboin vanquished in battle in 566. Even so, it remains somewhat strange that, having secured this victory, Alboin and the Lombards simply relinquished their lands to take up an invitation to enter Italy. Further, of course, one should not view the invitation of Narses as one that was designed to help the new Byzantine Emperor Justin II (565–578) secure and protect his Italian provinces; rather it was a response to the treatment Narses had experienced in his removal from military power. Alternatively, it could well have been an unprompted invasion initiated without any approval. In this light, with the consolidation of power by the Avars in Pannonia, it might be better to view the Lombards as refugees fleeing from a possible subjugation by their erstwhile allies against the Gepids. This might be a better explanation for Alboin's bestowal of Lombard Danubian lands before he departed to Italy. All this matters, of course, because it sheds some light on what happened and why that happened as the Lombards cross into *Venetia*.

This brings us to the second aspect we should tackle. Insufficient attention in this debate is focused on the conditions in the north of Italy in the 560s, prior to the Lombard advent. The so-called Copenhagen *Continuation of Prosper* simply notes (*s.a.* 1518) that Narses "having expelled the Goths...brought the people of all Italy back to their original joy." This judgement would appear to be rather too optimistic. As further reading of the *HL* and other sources demonstrates, the Lombards did not enter a vacuum, and in these early years they were forced to fight against Byzantine and Frankish forces, sometimes simultaneously. Indeed, it might not be entirely apposite to maintain that Frankish or Merovingian Italy ended in 561, 562, or even 565, because the Franks remained as significant protagonists in Italian affairs throughout the sixth and first half of the seventh centuries, even if formal territorial control was not maintained. As for the East Roman/Byzantine authorities and the Italo-Roman populations, one cannot depict a coordinated, let alone coherent, response to the advent of the Lombards. One is left without certainties.

A third aspect of our difficulties relates to the evidential platforms and narrative presentations of the period 568 to 572. The earliest sources, such as the *OgL* or the *Auctarium Havniensis Prosperi* (the Copenhagen *Continuation of Prosper*; hereafter *AHP*), are unhelpful in their terse and pithy statements. The *AHP*, for instance, states that Alboin "entered Italy with the whole Lombard people" and that they (improbably) "settled quietly in Italy."[1] Although Paul the Deacon's account

1 Steven Muhlberger, "The Copenhagen Continuation of Prosper: A Translation," *Florilegium* 6 (1984): 90.

is richer, it remains problematic, since it both simplifies and telescopes the events of these years. On the one hand, he records the capture of the fortress of *Forum Iulii* (modern Cividale del Friuli) and subsequently Vicenza and Verona, and the entry into *Mediolanum* (Milan) on September 3, 568, when all of "Liguria" (at this time comprised both modern *Lombardia* and Liguria) was captured. On the other hand, he notes that Padova, Monselice, and Mantova were not seized, and it took three years to capture Pavia. One must doubt his suggestion (in *HL* 2.26) that the Lombards "took possession of everything as far as Tuscany, except Rome and Ravenna."

Ultimately, whether we maintain that the Lombards were invaders- or poachers-turned-gamekeepers matters not considering the structural and logistical problems they encountered. Their physical control of the north of Italy was neither complete nor secure. More challenges were to come because of the murders of Alboin in 572 and of his successor Cleph in 574, which ushered in a period when there was no Lombard king in Pavia at all. The demise of Alboin is without doubt the most (in)famous episode in Lombard history and has generated numerous plays in Italian, English, and Swedish; at least two operas, modern novels and even a 1961 "sword and sandal" film in which Jack Palance portrayed Alboin and Eleonora Rossi Drago was Rosamunda. We shall not, however, dwell upon this episode at length here. Suffice to say that viewed in a wider perspective, the murder of Alboin prompted a period of active conflict between the Lombards and the Empire, which persisted for the next thirty years or so. The interregnum that followed from the death of Cleph in 574 marked a point when the Lombard dukes based in several Italian cities acted essentially as *condottieri* (mercenaries). Some of the dukes allied themselves with the Empire, some did not, and some switched sides repeatedly. This was probably the point at which the Lombard dukedoms of Spoleto in the centre of Italy and Benevento further south were first created by Faroald I (570–591/2) and Zotto (571–591), respectively, who acted independently of both Imperial and Lombard authority. The situation was to remain fluid, even febrile, right across the ten years of the interregnum and through the rule of Authari, whose election as Lombard king was propelled by the threat of a Frankish and Imperial alliance designed to extinguish the Lombards entirely.

Revival, 590–616

The death of Authari and his replacement by Agilulf signal the point when the Lombard Kingdom attained a solidity and a strength to resist external pressures and to coerce the regional elites into submission. Agilulf's efforts across nearly three decades represent a revival, if not reformulation, of the Kingdom. According to Paul the Deacon (*HL* 3.35), Agilulf was not only "energetic and warlike" but also "fitted as well in body as in mind for the government of the kingdom." The somewhat unstable state of Lombard governance and the key relationships between Pavia and the dukes in their localities was the first and most immediate challenge that Agilulf had to address. During just one chapter of book 4 of the *HL*, Paul the Deacon records three dukes who resisted the king's authority. One was put to death for surrendering to the Franks previously. Another fortified his city, was besieged, made peace, but then fled and "shut himself up in the island of Comacina" before being captured and (surprisingly) forgiven. The third was likewise besieged and then captured. A little time later (probably ca. 597) Gaidulf of Bergamo, who had been forgiven twice, was slain along with Zangrulf of Verona and Warnecaut of Pavia, who had all rebelled against Agilulf. By ca. 602 or 603, Agilulf was powerful enough to persuade both Gaidoald of Trent and Gisulf of *Forum Iulii* (ca. 590–610) to make peace and accept his authority.

Challenge to the Kingdom also came from external powers. The topsy-turvy and interminable tapestry of conflict between the Lombards and the Empire had persisted throughout the time of the interregnum and Authari, complicated by a shifting horizon of alliance and counter-alliance that crossed political and ethnic affiliations. Thus, Maurisio, a *dux* in Perugia, "had gone over to the side of the Romans" along with a set of strongpoints that linked Rome and Ravenna. Agilulf's resolute action included attacking Perugia and killing Maurisio (d. 593/4) and then destroying Padova. Later, we are told, Agilulf set out from Milan, captured Cremona, assaulted Mantova with battering rams, and, having captured this city, moved onwards to assail *Vulturina* and Brescello. All this seems to have collectively put the Empire on the back foot and resulted in an agreed truce for nine months.

One should not allow the patterning of Paul the Deacon's *HL* narrative, however, to obscure the fact that the Lombard Kingdom was not preoccupied by the Empire alone. Both the adjacent Franks and Avars posed serious, if not existential, threats to the Kingdom's serenity. To tackle these neighbours, Agilulf agreed "a perpetual peace with the Avars." Subsequently, and in concert with the Avars, the Lombards invaded Istria and "laid waste everything with burnings and plunderings" (*HL* 4.24). As part of the perpetual peace, the Avar ambassador travelled to Gaul and admonished the Franks to keep peace with the Lombards. The relationship with the Franks was complicated, and for significant parts of the early seventh century the Lombards were held in a tributary relationship. Fredegar explained in his chronicle, written closer in time to the events than Paul the Deacon's account, that the Lombards "had placed themselves without reserve under Frankish overlordship" to avoid further difficulties caused by Lombard raids into Gaul. Both Authari, who Fredegar emphasized was chosen with Frankish permission, and Agilulf paid an annual tribute of twelve thousand *solidi*. In this context, it is entirely understandable why, when Authari died in 590, that messengers were sent to Childebert II (575–596) to seek acceptance of Agilulf as king. Later, Agilulf secured peace with Childebert's son Theuderic II (596–613), which permitted Agilulf to pursue his military activities against the Empire without fear of invasion from the north. Fredegar's narrative account of Agilulf's contacts with the Franks, whilst it errs in its chronological context, explains how the Lombard Kingdom extricated itself from the onerous financial burden of tribute by bribing the mayors of the palace and paying three years of tribute at once. The Lombards were then excused tribute, and a "pact of eternal friendship" was agreed. The Franks thus mollified, Agilulf could concentrate on the situation in Italy itself.

Agilulf's agreement to several truces with the Empire signalled more than simply an acceptance of a stalemate where neither protagonist was strong enough to "knock" the other out. It also gave him the necessary impetus to collate the local "power-groups," as Chris Wickham called them, into the Kingdom's orbit. Even with an effective ruler such as Agilulf, such connection remained a series of individual relationships based on clienteles, an uncertain balance between centre and the regions, and, for the dukes and their followers, some independence of action. Throughout the Kingdom's existence, the power balance between kings in Pavia (usually) and the dukes remained fluid, occasionally unstable, and always one in which the king had to tread carefully. At least three (possibly four) of these areas, i.e., Friuli, Spoleto, and Benevento (even Trent(o), which may certainly be said to have been autonomous in the period before Agilulf) maintained elevated levels of geopolitical autonomy, but even smaller power-centres, such as Trent(o), Asti, Brescia, and Turin, could furnish dukes with ambitions to challenge for the kingship. So far as one can tell, Agilulf's policy was one of "carrot and stick." We have already seen his reported indulgence regarding Gaidulf of Bergamo, but this was spliced with his ruthless treatment of opponents, termed rebels by Paul the Deacon. The specific mechanics of governance at this time remain rather obscure, for we lack the sort of administrative documentation that would shed light on day-to-day activities. Yet there are hints from several aspects of his rule that suggest that Agilulf attempted to imitate or cultivate an Italo-Lombard regime in a similar fashion to Theoderic the Great's fusion of Ostrogoths and Romans in the sixth century. These are cumulatively, however, only hints at a broader strategy allied to peace with external powers and control of elite groups beyond Pavia. Paul the Deacon's short notices on court culture hints at this broader policy with reference to the

Figure 5. The Lamina of Agilulf. Gilt bronze. Florence, Museo Bargello. Photograph by Saliko. Wikimedia Commons. CC BY-SA 3.0.

foundation of churches by Agilulf's queen, Theodelinda, and the presence of Secundus of Non at the court when baptizing Adaloald in Monza as well as later, when Adaloald was elevated as king in the circus of Milan (incidentally in the presence of Frankish ambassadors). Perhaps most evocative is the so-called Lamina of Agilulf (Figure 5). Housed today at the Museo Bargello in Firenze, the gilt bronze lamina, a part of a helmet plate, depicts the king (identifiable by the inscription: *DN AG IL V REGI*) seated on a throne guarded by warriors on each side and angels with signs declaring *victuria*. Whilst there is no clear scholarly consensus on what the scene actually portrays, it should also be noted that in an article from 2010, Stefano Gasparri and Cristina La Rocca were equivocal about the item's authenticity.

Agilulf's tenure of kingship by any standard was indeed effective, as Paul the Deacon suggested, and at his death it was robust enough for him to pass on rule to his wife Theodelinda and their son Adaloald (616–626).

Retrenchment and Resilience, 616–671

Having saved the Kingdom of the Lombards from dissolution by a pincer movement between the Empire and the Franks, the first half of the seventh century is a relatively obscure period to follow. Narrative sources are unsatisfactory and do not adequately provide answers to the sort of questions that fascinate us today. This is a pity for the processes of cohesion and development between the death of Agilulf in 616, and the assumption of power of Rothari twenty years later are entirely opaque, but, of course, also fundamental in understanding how the Lombards' political enterprise weathered external challenges and moulded an enduring socio-political community. One might venture to say, however, that the idiom of Lombard kingship as constructed by Agilulf, which seemed to emphasize an Italo-Roman aspect, was replaced by a more robust Lombard idiom of power which defined itself in tension with Byzantium. This is clearly enunciated by Rothari, as we shall see below, in the promulgation of Lombard law and contained in the text of the *OgL*. Reading between the lines in the *HL* and the pertinent sections of Fredegar's work, now that Agilulf was in his grave, one acquires an impression that Theodelinda (and Adaloald) attempted to steer a closer relationship with the Empire which also involved some form of religious rapprochement with Rome. Paul the Deacon discharges the ten years or so in one brief notice but does point out that under their rule "churches were restored, and many gifts were bestowed upon the holy places." Adaloald was removed from power, he adds, due to insanity (*HL* 4.41). His notice, however, poses very many more questions than it could ever answer. Historians are not known to like vacuums, and into this absence of detail theories were constructed, such as by Gian-Piero Bognetti (1902–1963), which explained the development of the Kingdom as a tussle between two competing factions. We considered some of these aspects in the chapter above on religion. In terms of political elites, such competition was viewed as revolving around a faction that favoured an "Arian" religious orientation linked into an expression of kingship that saw the king as no more than first amongst equals and an opposing group who preferred a more orthodox policy where the kings were stronger and compelled greater obedience. Naturally, there is simplification here, but the broad tendrils of the idea, having flowed from the great Italian historian Bognetti, remained influential beyond their evidential utility, until they were effectively debunked by the works of Steven Fanning, T. S. Brown, and Piero Majocchi.

Not only does Fredegar, who compiled his chronicle in the third quarter of the seventh century, have more to say, he also provides greater detail which casts some doubt on Paul's presentation.[2] Fredegar maintained that Adaloald had fallen foul of a Byzantine plot in which a certain Eusebius had persuaded the king to use an ointment in his bath. This unguent allowed Eusebius to constrain the king's will to his own, to suggest that all the "great men" of the Lombards should be killed and then the Kingdom delivered up to the emperor. Having dispatched twelve of their brethren, the surviving Lombard lords elected Arioald (called Charoald in Fredegar) as king, and Adaloald was poisoned and replaced.[3] Arioald, it should also be noted, had married the sister of Adaloald, Gundeperga (ca. 600–ca. after 653), who, akin to her mother, was to be later instrumental in the transmission of power to Arioald's successor, Rothari. Whilst Fredegar first suggests that Arioald was elected unanimously, he does report a rebellion by a certain Taso, *dux* of Lombard *Tuscia* (we shall set aside the problematic existence of a *dux* in *Tuscia*), and, in a long notice on the probity of Gundeperga, a link is made between the queen and the rebel. At the very least we can suggest that the transmission of power in the Kingdom at this time remained uncertain and contested, and such current flowed throughout the rest of the seventh century. Both Arioald and Rothari, Fredegar tells us, imprisoned Gundeperga, the former for alleged infidelity and collusion with Taso and the latter for her popularity since "all the Lombards had sworn her fealty." What emerges from the lengthy notices we have is that Gundeperga and, indeed, her mother, Theodelinda,

---

2 Christopher Heath, *The Narrative Worlds of Paul the Deacon: Between Empires and Identities in Lombard Italy* (Amsterdam University Press, 2017), 205–6.

3 Wallace-Hadrill, *Fourth book of the Chronicle of Fredegar*, 41.

were significantly more important than subsequent synthetic narratives of Italian history allow, but we remain somewhat restricted by what we are told by commentators and how they framed their notices.

This remains a problem for our perceptions of Rothari and his successors, Aripert I (653–661) and Grimoald. Certainly, concerning Rothari, and setting aside his contribution to Lombard law, one might think that developments in his time were rather limited and restricted to a renewal of offensive military campaigns against the Byzantine Empire. In these efforts the king had some success. In the first place, he conquered Liguria, although Fredegar emphasizes that he destroyed the cities on the coast and "left them in flames." Second, further east he destroyed *Opitergium* (now Oderzo) and defeated the Empire at the battle of Scultenna in 636. It might be an exaggeration to suggest that these activities put the Lombard Kingdom "on-the-front-foot" in Italy, particularly as Oderzo was re-occupied by the Empire, but they do hint at a renewed confidence on the part of Pavia, as it progressively nibbled away at Imperial territory throughout Italy. Such attritional warfare seems to have continued under Grimoald, who had supplanted the sons of Aripert I in 662. Judgements on Grimoald are also difficult to make and entirely reliant on the observations of Paul the Deacon. The late Walter Goffart in his seminal *Narrators of Barbarian History* of 1988, for instance, was sure that for Paul the Deacon Grimoald was the prime epitome of Lombard kingship. Yet a careful examination of what we are told reveals a rather more ambivalent response to his rule. The broader picture demonstrates that enmity and military activity between the Lombards and the Empire continued, and the field of conflict expanded to include Benevento. This was where Emperor Constans II (641–668) had made what proved to be the final attempt of Byzantium to attain hegemony throughout Italy. Grimoald had been the *dux* in Benevento, and his assistance to his son, Romuald I (662–687), proved instrumental in resisting Constans' effort to take over the south of Italy. More problematic in terms of success or failure were Grimoald's relations with his neighbours, the Avars to the east and the Franks to the west. Having importuned the Avars to invade Friuli and deal with the ambitious *dux* Lupus, he could not convince his erstwhile allies to return home without convincing them that his hastily collected army was an immense multitude. Similarly, whilst Grimoald defeats a Frankish army at the so-called Brook of the Franks, it seems to have been part of the disturbances that arose from his usurpation of kingship from Aripert's sons. The curious epitaph Paul the Deacon composes emphasizes Grimoald's bodily strength combined with his wisdom, which seems to be at odds with some of the reports Paul provides about the king previously.

With his death, Grimoald's old adversary Perctarit returns to the centre of Lombard events. Whilst it might not have appeared to have been a dramatic change at the time, for historians looking back this was a pivotal event. Perctarit's kingship in concert with his son Cunincpert marked a turning point in the expression and use of Lombard power. For this crucial period, we are nearly entirely dependent upon the notices that Paul the Deacon furnishes. Whilst we have no reason to think that Paul has invented his information, his presentation of material and the framework which he deploys must prompt some care as to what we conclude and extract from his narrative. Even so, several significant developments may be traced. First, there is apparent peace with the Byzantine Empire. Thomas Brown has reminded us of the flimsy evidential foundation for believing that there was a formal peace made in 680, but, despite this, we have no indication that active hostilities were commenced or persisted. This also seems to be the case with both the Franks and the Avars. Second, internal tensions persisted with a rebellion by Alahis, whom Paul designated as a "son of iniquity," being the prime example during Perctarit's kingship. The notices we possess dwell upon personalities and how Perctarit's son Cunincpert persuaded his father not only to forgive Alahis his opposition but even to bestow upon him the dukedom of Brescia, closer to the central seat of Lombard power. Third, there are a few hints in the *HL* that Perctarit linked his kingship into a closer connection with the Church and sought to express the idiom of kingship through that connection. At his death in 688, the kingship transferred to Cunincpert seamlessly, partly because the latter had been associated with kingship from 680. Yet there was soon trouble ahead, because Alahis once again sought kingship and succeeded in supplanting Cunincpert for the best part of a year. Alahis did not prove to be a successful usurper and was in turn defeated and replaced by Cunincpert after a battle at the river Adda.

The trends initiated by Perctarit strengthen in the twelve years of Cunincpert's sole rule, although once again one must extrapolate from the sole witness of the *HL*. One lesson that flows from the Alahis episode is that the key dynamic in the Lombard Kingdom remained that between Pavia and the regions, where, for the most part, the king's power was mediated through local elites headed by dukes, bishops, and *gastalds*. The latter ostensibly acted as the king's eyes and ears in the regions but in practice could be related to the local duke and entirely co-opted into that network. Regional loyalties based on cities is a feature of the Alahis episode and comes to the fore in the instabilities that flowed after the death of Cunincpert. This feature of the Lombard body politic may help us to understand the brutal suppression of opposition that Paul the Deacon mentions. Ansfrit of Ragogna, for instance, usurped the dukedom of Friuli and, in a pattern familiar on previous occasions, rebelled against Cunincpert but was seized in Verona, blinded, and exiled. Despite the insecurities of rule, the key theme of this period is the robust integrity of the Kingdom which withstood these rebellions, so that ultimately Cunincpert could leave his kingdom to his son Liutpert.

Hegemony, Hubris, and Downfall, 701–774

Boy kings in the Early Middle Ages did not tend to prosper. Of the three examples in the Lombard Kingdom, only Adaloald in the early seventh century survived beyond a year or so. Cunincpert had entrusted his young son into the care of

Ansprand, who is described as Liutpert's tutor. This was to prove insufficient in the febrile conditions of conflict that soon followed. Of the six contenders for supremacy, only the victors Raginpert and his son Aripert and the defeated Ansprand survived. With the death of Raginpert within a year, his son Aripert emerged victorious and unchallenged further. It is difficult to know what to make of Aripert II (701–712) since we depend almost entirely upon the *HL* (with a brief reference in the Frankish *Vita Boniti episcopi Arverni*). Foulke's dry remark in his English translation of the *HL* that "Paul's estimate of Aripert's character is evidently too favourable" is based upon the internal evidence supplied by Paul himself. Paul suggests that Aripert was a "religious man, given to charities and a lover of justice," but he follows this remark with the observation that whilst there was "very great fertility of the land," the times were "barbarous." When one scrutinizes the narrative for details, however, the impression formed is that Aripert's tenure as king was not one in which he felt secure. We are told that he would lurk around at night and ask what was said about him and that when foreign ambassadors appeared, he would try to appear poorly dressed and ensure that no precious wines nor "delicacies of other kinds" would be offered (*HL* 6.35). Such behaviour was to avail Aripert little protection from an invasion from the north, when Ansprand, his son Liutprand, and a force of Bavarians appeared before Pavia. In a hard-fought encounter Ansprand was to prevail. At this stage in the life of the Lombard Kingdom, no one might anticipate the trajectory the young Liutprand would take.

Whilst it is hazardous to judge specific rulers as the most powerful or most significant of any given polity, a consensus has formed around the rule of Liutprand. Whether he was "energetic" or a "lover of peace" or not, his contribution to the Lombard Kingdom was fundamental beyond the thirty-two years of his rule, and he provided a basic imprint for his successors, Ratchis, Aistulf, and Desiderius. Neil Christie's formula in his entry in the *Oxford Dictionary of Late Antiquity* is perhaps the best precis of Liutprand's career. We have already discussed his legal impact in the promulgation of laws above, but to this we should add, following Christie, his religious patronage and his military activity. Both elements reflect the fruitful splicing of the prominent aspects of Lombard kingship embodied by his predecessors, notably Agilulf and Rothari in terms of military effectiveness and Perctarit and Cunincpert in their religious orientation. Whilst Liutprand's rule first encounters the usual forms of elite opposition, his early promulgation of law sets the agenda for his subsequent rule that binds local elite networks into a capillary structure of governance and increasingly intrudes Pavia into the Kingdom's regions, such as Friuli. For the first time we also see Liutprand bring both Spoleto and Benevento to heal. The former is closely subjugated and controlled; the latter is linked into the power network of Pavia, albeit loosely. The result is that by the 730s the Lombard Kingdom had attained a hegemonic position in the Italian peninsula. There remained, however, two interlinked problems, consequent to geographical infelicity that the Lombard kings were never to entirely resolve.

The first of these issues involved their near neighbours on the peninsula. The Exarchate of Ravenna, the Byzantine Empire, and the Papacy were all subject to the authority of Constantinople, but one consequence of the iconoclastic crisis in Italy was the increasing autonomy of the popes in Rome. All these protagonists, together with Spoleto and Benevento, were connected into Liutprand's plans and at one time or another sought to form alliance and counter-alliance to thwart Pavia's ambitions. Liutprand had recommenced offensive military operations against the Empire in the mid-720s, but these were rather piecemeal activities. There had been up to that point a lengthy peace between the Empire and the Lombards in the north, but the iconoclastic troubles had thrown Byzantine Italy into tumult, and it is attractive to think that Liutprand took advantage of the instabilities unleashed. He has been seen in some scholarship as an opportunist, but this would be to underestimate the careful implementation of policy on his part. By 737, Liutprand's military activities permitted the capture of Bologna, where he formed a new Lombard dukedom based on Persiceta. On two occasions he captured the whole of the Exarchate, as he then moved onwards to deal with the Spoletan *duces* who had tried to play the Lombard Kingdom off against the pope and the Exarchate. The tapestry of events is complicated and has aptly been called a *danse macabre* by Jeffrey Richards, but one can certainly see that Liutprand's military imperative to connect the Kingdom proper to Spoleto occasioned a need for security to the north, i.e., Ravenna. It is evident that Liutprand did not have territorial ambitions in respect of Rome and was pragmatic about the small remnant of the Exarchate that remained, but he needed to be able to constrain Spoleto effectively. His ambitions, however, were circumscribed by the popes. As we saw in the discussion of belief in Lombard Italy, Liutprand deferred to the religious and moral authority of the papacy and could not turn this deference to his political advantage. In fact, during his final meeting with Pope Zacharias (741–752) his hand was forced, and he was obliged to return territory both to Rome and the Exarchate. This issue was left entirely unresolved at his death in March 744.

The second issue was the Frankish kingdoms to the north. Liutprand and his immediate predecessors had been saved the unwelcome attention the Kingdom had previously received from the Franks earlier in the seventh century. Liutprand, as Paul the Deacon emphasized in his remarkable encomium for the king, always kept peace with the Franks or at least allied himself with their leader, Charles Martel (715–741). Both rulers benefitted from the alliance. In the first place, they both intervened in Bavaria, to their mutual benefit. Second, Liutprand provided material assistance to Charles when Gaul and Provence were invaded by "Saracens," although Liutprand's army is not known to have undertaken any fighting. In practical terms, this meant that Liutprand was left a free hand to develop his plans in Italy. Thus, when Gregory III (731–741) appealed to Charles Martel for help, he advised Charles in a letter from late 739 or early 740 not to believe "the fraudulent cajoleries and inducements" of Liutprand (and his nephew Hildeprand), who write "trickeries that their dukes...of Spoleto and Benevento have committed some so-called wrong against them."[4] Gregory implored Charles to "not scorn my pleas, please do not close off your ears to my request: thus, may the prince of the apostles not close off the heavenly kingdom to you." Gregory sent a further (extant) letter, but neither generated any intervention.

Gregory was thus left without assistance, but the issues for the papacy did not evaporate and were to return to the forefront across the next thirty years. The death of Liutprand marks a watershed moment in the sources at our disposal, because the *HL* of Paul the Deacon ends with the death of the former. For the last three kings, we are left with an imperfect combination of (often) hostile and biased materials, not least the *Codex epistolaris Carolinus* and the *LP*, the first compiled for a specific Frankish audience and the latter edited and curated for a papal perspective. Continuations of Paul the Deacon, the histories of Andrew of Bergamo and of Erchempert of Benevento do not fill the gap. Consequently, much of the standard narratives on the last three Lombard kings concentrate on relations with external powers, most notably the Franks, the Bavarians, and the Papacy. Evidence for what is going on within the Kingdom can be found in additions to Lombard law made by Ratchis and Aistulf and with pertinent charters. Yet, all told, we are left to extrapolate from hints and materials that are often rather odd bedfellows.

Ratchis and his brother Aistulf embodied two different approaches to the challenges left to them by Liutprand. Ratchis in his prologue to his laws of 746 emphasized his connections to Liutprand, whom he described as "that most glorious and orthodox supporter of the faith and ruler of this nation, and, through the mercy of omnipotent God, our instructor" (Drew, 218). The *LP*, which provides an episodic (and often highly partial) narrative of some events in Italy, references Ratchis as setting out to capture Perugia in 749

4 *Codex epistolaris Carolinus: Letters from the Popes to the Frankish Rulers 739–91*, ed. Rosamund McKitterick et al. (Liverpool University Press, 2021), 149.

in "a mighty fury." The pope at this time, Zacharias had successfully turned Liutprand's military efforts to peace in 744, and he did the same on this occasion when he persuaded Ratchis to abandon the siege.[5] This decision seems to have prompted the removal of Ratchis from kingship by his brother, rather than, as the *LP* would have it, that Ratchis moved by the spiritual prayer of the pope sought to enter a life of religious devotion with his wife, Tassia, and their children. The chronology between the end of the siege in Perugia and the removal of Ratchis is important but not possible to pin down with certainty. In any case, at an assembly in Milan in July 749 Aistulf was elected to replace Ratchis.

Hints at conflict between the two brothers, and, consequentially, the right approach to Italian events is given by the laws of Aistulf, which pointedly rescind the gifts and donations of Ratchis and family unless they are validated once more by Aistulf himself. Usually the younger brother of Ratchis has been portrayed as more "forceful" and, certainly, firmly opposed to the popes and to the Franks. Of course, it remains difficult to ascribe to the brothers entrenched positions based on being either anti- or pro-Roman. Whilst Ratchis may have self-consciously adopted Liutprand's approach; in fact it was Aistulf who embodied a more robust version of Liutprand's policies. Once again, he subjugated Spoleto and ruled this directly, brought Benevento back into the orbit of the Kingdom, and extinguished the Byzantine Exarchate of Ravenna in 751. However, the problem for him, as for his brother and, indeed, Desiderius who followed on, was that the situation in Francia had shifted. The newly minted king of the Franks, Pippin I (751–768) viewed himself as the protector of the papacy and the guarantor of their safety from Lombard hegemony now that, for all intents and purposes, the Byzantine emperors could no longer furnish any effective assistance. Aistulf's successes have been occluded by

5 R. Davis, *The Lives of the Eighth-Century Popes (Liber Pontificalis)* (Liverpool University Press, 2007), 46–47.

the *damnatio memoriae* he suffered at the hands of the *LP*, wherein he is variously described as "shameless," "cruel," "criminal," and "pestilential." His "pernicious savagery," however, was restrained by two Frankish military interventions which forced Aistulf to return his conquests and to accept, on the second occasion, Frankish supervision of his activities. Before any further interventions could occur, however, Aistulf died due to a hunting accident in December 756.

It is perhaps a paradox that Desiderius attained Lombard kingship, partially because of papal approbation. In the end, both the king and his kingdom were undone by the popes and their alliance with the newly minted Carolingian kings of Francia. This does not mean, however, that Desiderius was not alive to the challenges the Lombards faced. In his seventeen years as Lombard king Desiderius demonstrated a dexterity that belies his position as the last Lombard king of the Lombards. In the construction of a new *Ehepolitik*, where three of his daughters were married to neighbouring rulers, he sought to expand his influence, so that the Franks could be constrained and permit him to embark on a renewed effort to attain a hegemonic position in the peninsula. For the latter, he attained similar success to Aistulf. He removed Alboin as *dux* of Spoleto and first directly controlled Spoleto before nominating dukes himself; in Benevento he replaced the *dux* Liutprand (749–758), who had allied with the Franks, with Liutprand's son, Arechis II (758–787), to whom his daughter Adelperga was married. Efforts to entangle the papacy into a Lombard hegemony were, despite considerable intrigue and expense, to prove ineffective and ultimately prompted a further appeal to the Franks for assistance. When Charlemagne invaded Italy in 773, Desiderius attempted to use the old and usually successful tactic of retirement behind the city walls of Pavia. Presumably the thinking here would have been that the Franks would tire of besieging the city and return to Francia after perhaps attaining some form of financial or political recompense. Whilst this worked on several occasions in the sixth century, it was not successful in the eighth century. In fact, Lombard dukes did not repel the invasion or challenge the siege and instead submitted to the Franks. Pavia surrendered in 774, and Desiderius was taken into exile. Verona, where the son of Desiderius, Adelgis, had found refuge, surrendered without resistance and Adelgis, who was—in the words of Paul the Deacon's epitaph to Queen Ansa, the wife of Desiderius—to be the *spes* (hope) of the Lombard people, fled to Constantinople. In the dry words of the chronicler of the *Continuatio Romana*, the Lombard Kingdom of 206 years' duration had ended.

Chapter 5

Langobardia Minor: The Lombard *Mezzogiorno*, 774–1077

With the end of the siege of Pavia in 774, the capture of Desiderius and his exile to Francia—an independent Lombard polity in the north and centre of the peninsula—ended definitively. Two years later the revolt of Hrodgaud of Friuli (d. 776) failed. The focus of Lombard political life thus shifts to the south, where the former duchy of Benevento weathered the challenge of ascendant Frankish power but sought to retain its own effective independence. *Dux* Arechis of Benevento (758–787) adopted the title of prince and thus signalled his intent to continue the long tradition of Beneventan autonomy from the north. Arechis, like those that ruled in Benevento and the south thereafter, found themselves caught between the ascendant power of the Franks and that of the Byzantine Empire. Playing one emperor against another was never a comfortable approach, as the events of 788 and later demonstrated. The intricacies between powers within and without the peninsula and the instabilities they unleashed in Benevento is a recurrent theme of this period. In 1907, René Poupardin's *Études sur l'historie des principautés lombardes de l'Italie méridionale* dismissed this region and its history as a "story of internecine struggles, as fruitless as it was obscure." For the eminent historian Ferdinand Chalandon (1875–1921), as stated in his 1907 work *Histoire de la domination normande en Italie et en Sicile*, there was "nothing more monotonous than the continual wars between the Lombard princes and their neighbours." Recent engagement with the region maintains an entirely different view without pejorative judgements on the complex struggles for authority which are a feature of events.

This chapter will trace the Lombard tradition in the south through significant changes that included the progressive fragmentation of Benevento in the ninth century into first two, then three polities, i.e., Benevento, Salerno, and Capua. During the long tenth century (ca. 880–ca. 1030), Capua and Benevento often shared the same ruler, the best example of which was the evocatively named Pandulf Ironhead (943–981), who reunited the remaining Lombard lands in the south under the theoretical tutelage of the Ottonian emperors. Yet, within a century of his death in 981, all three Lombard entities had been taken over by the Normans. Landulf VI's death in 1077 marks the political end of Lombard Italy. The three hundred years we shall consider here are not well known in Anglophone historical scholarship and suffer (certainly from 999 onwards) with the taint of hindsight, since it is difficult to avoid analysis that is not coloured with the knowledge of ultimate Norman success. Whilst there will be no year-by-year account, engagement with *Langobardia Minor*, the Lombard *Mezzogiorno*, should be considered in a wider context that links it back to the Kingdom in Pavia and also for its role as a crucial site of transregional contact. It is, indeed, a case study in the limits and possibilities of power in the Early Middle Ages. Let us return to Arechis and 774.

Reinvention and Resilience, 774–849

It is doubtful that Arechis II, the *dux* of Benevento, viewed the end of the Lombard Kingdom in the north in 774 with serenity. Despite his intent, when he nominated himself as *princeps* of the Lombard people, and his assertion that he legislated for the "salvation and justice of this country," the Beneventans had to walk a tightrope between autonomy and subservience to the new Frankish masters. Later, by the time of Adelchis (853–878) in the ninth century, a sense of indomitable resilience against the odds could be expressed in the preface to his law. "Celestial piety" had committed the province to Adelchis whilst his people were "gravely under threat from a multitude of peoples who do not cease to terrify and dispossess our fellow citizens, burning and sacking many of our villages and towns."[1] This dramatic view of the Lombard ninth century was echoed by our principal source from the period, the *History of the Lombards who Live in Benevento* (hereafter *HLdB*) of Erchempert of Benevento (*fl.* 840s–880s). Erchempert's narrative has received considerable attention recently, not least because his work remains the main (but not only) source for *Langobardia Minor* in the ninth century. Viewing the Lombards through this source alone is not without problems of perspective and focus. Erchempert's prologue, for instance, whilst linking his work into a tradition of Italian historical writing commenced by Paul the Deacon, aimed to tell "not their [i.e., the Lombards] domination, but their end, not their happiness, but their misery, not their triumph, but their ruin." Since we essentially only know Erchempert through his narrative, he remains a fascinating figure, although he is sometimes rather opaque in his responses to the events he portrays. Whilst he has been called a "reluctant fustigator" by Luigi Andrea Berto, there are occasions when the gloom one might expect to encounter in his work is lifted. The treatment of events, however, is not balanced with a bias towards Benevento and Capua to the detriment of Salerno. Similarly, Erchempert concentrates on military and dynastic matters and rarely provides the reader with the sort of colourful anecdotes and narratives that feature in Paul the Deacon's *HL* or even in the later *Chronicon Salernitanum*. Also sidelined, and usually demonized, are the Islamic protagonists that we encounter in the *HLdB*. It can be difficult, then, to avoid replicating the imprint of Erchempert when analyzing the period between 774 and 889, when his work ends. Luckily, as noted above, Erchempert's work can be supplemented on occasion with other materials which

1 Everett, *Literacy in Lombard Italy*, 97.

help to provide a more rounded view. Recently, this overall picture has reintegrated the Islamic contribution to events in the south, but this forms part of the kaleidoscope in the *Mezzogiorno* from the ninth century, in particular.

This kaleidoscope is much more than just Benevento alone. As we progress through the late eighth and early ninth centuries, three sets of protagonists, exterior to the Lombards, assume increasing significance for geopolitical matters. We have already noted the Frankish dimension which looms over the Beneventan elite for the seventy years from 774, to which should be added the residual presence of the Byzantine Empire, which was on the defensive in Sicily with the ongoing Aghlabid Islamic amirate's attritional conquests from 827 onwards and also present in modern Calabria and the *Terra d'Otranto*, at the heel of modern Puglia. Of course, we cannot forget the increasing role of Islamic polities and protagonists on the mainland based in Taranto and Bari, the latter of which is traditionally said to have been created in ca. 847. In this dizzying array of interests, polities, and protagonists it is rather difficult sometimes to see the wood for the trees, but a clear impression that the Beneventan Lombards are in trouble is inescapable. Instead of trudging through the miasma of detail, we shall now consider three "moments" in the pivotal seventy years after 774: first, the rule of Arechis II and his son Grimoald III (787–806); second, the regime of Sico I (817–832) and his son, Sicard (832–839); and, third, as a prelude to the division of Benevento, the rule of Radelchis I (839–851).

Arechis II and his son Grimoald III represent the bridge between the Lombard idiom of power as expressed in Pavia for the better part of two hundred years as well as the transplanted tradition in Benevento. The significant cultural production of the court of Arechis demonstrates this link, perhaps a self-conscious one but one not based alone on the local rulers of Benevento who went back to Zotto (571–591) at the end of the sixth century or any of his successors who had kept the Kingdom at arm's length. Just as the kingship of Liutprand had embodied two strands of a political inheritance, so too did Benevento, which maintained its own autonomy but connected that back into the longer Lombard past. In this way, beyond political efforts to square the circle of Frankish interventions but retain sufficient scope for independent action, Arechis and his wife, Adelperga, daughter of Desiderius (ca. 740–after 787), presided over a court that initiated several significant projects which emphasized that connection. This is most notably reflected in important works of Paul the Deacon, such as his *Historia Romana* and his poetry in honour of Arechis, after his death. On a more concrete level, Arechis oversaw the construction of Santa Sofia in Benevento and the foundation of Salerno as the second seat of Beneventan power. Zornetta, in her *Italia meridionale longobarda: Competizione, conflitto e potere politico a Benevento*, observed that it was not possible to identify internal tensions within Benevento at this time. This does not mean, however, that the socio-political environment of Benevento was an unlikely oasis of serenity in a sea of medieval discord. Earlier, in the 740s, there had been a lengthy dispute between the monastery of San Vincenzo al Volturno and a *gastald* named Radoald, and others, over land in Isernia. This dispute rumbled on through the rule of three Beneventan dukes. Even so, in terms of future development, signs of internal division, whilst not apparent during the rule of Arechis II, soon appear. This is interesting given the scope for the formation of groups affected by exterior influence who might or might not favour one particular power (in this case the Frankish or Byzantine empires). Yet the strain of keeping the Franks at bay tilted the Beneventan political elite into discord and disunity. This discordant scenario was best exemplified by the murder of Grimoald IV (806–817), the former *stolesayz* (treasurer) of Grimoald III described by Erchempert as "very gentle" and "so sweet" that he even made a peace agreement with the Neapolitans.[2] In 817, however, after three separate attempts to replace him, he was murdered by Radelchis of Conza and Sico, the *gastald* of Acerenza.

2 Berto, *Little History of the Lombards*, 89.

Sico's regime and, subsequently, his son Sicard's were not to prove as stable. This sets the agenda for a plethora of difficulties in the Lombard *Mezzogiorno* from this point onwards. Originally from the northeast of Italy, Sico and his family had intended (so we are told) to move into exile in Constantinople, save for a chance encounter with Grimoald IV, who appointed Sico *gastald* of Acerenza (nowadays in the modern region of Basilicata, adjacent to the border with Campania). The murder of Grimoald IV undertaken by Radelchis and Sico was a grim foretaste of future developments. Erchempert, who tends to yield to rather more hyperbolic language than Paul the Deacon, noted that Sico renewed a treaty with the Franks, so that he could treat the Beneventans with "bestial cruelty." Worse, he appointed his eldest son, Sicard, as heir, a man Erchempert described as "false, turbulent, petulant and arrogant." Once he had succeeded his father in 832, Sicard's "bestial voracity" against his own subjects demonstrated that "for the first time God's wrath has been unleashed to damn the Earth."[3] Yet it is rather more difficult to simply accept these statements at face value. Behind the scenes, and together with statements made in the later *Chronicon Salernitanum*, it is evident that there is an ongoing realignment of political factions. Sico used his family as a mechanism to extend his influence, with one son, Orso, made *gastald* of Conza and another, Radelmondo, *gastald* of Acerenza; a daughter Sicholenda was married to Azzone of Lucera; and Sicard himself married Adelchisa, the daughter of Dauferio "*il Balbo/il Muto*." Despite this, Erchempert emphasizes the malign influence of Roffrit, the son of Dauferius *il Propheta,* who, he suggested, persuaded Sicard to condemn his own brother Siconulf to "perpetual exile." The Beneventan political elite then remained in a state of discord throughout the 830s and into the 840s, even prior to the civil war that followed on from the death of Sicard in 839, at which point Siconulf escaped imprisonment and opposed the rule of Radelchis I.

3 Berto, *Little History of the Lombards*, 93.

The intricacies of the long civil war between Radelchis I and Siconulf, and the growing, independent importance of Capua under Landulf I the Old (840–843) need not detain us here. There are, however, two important points to make. First, in the division of loyalties caused by the conflict, it is evident that neither entity was sufficiently strong enough to "knock out" the other. Both looked to external protagonists for assistance and in so doing permitted Islamic mercenaries to acquire a significant presence in the south. Second, the formal division of Benevento sponsored by Emperor Louis II (844–875) in 849 signalled a new reality where southern rulers used (if not needed) exterior forces to enhance and maintain their legitimacy. A brief period when Benevento had been able to successfully adopt offensive campaigns against Naples under Grimoald IV and Sico ended and was replaced with one where the separate entities relied upon shifting alliances to maintain their existence against a background of instability and uncertainty. In this maelstrom of discord both Frankish and Islamic protagonists could play one side against the other but act for their own benefit. Whilst it might appear that the Lombards were on the back foot, their political dexterity stood them in good stead for the new realities on the ground.

Jeux lombardes: No More Heroes Anymore, 849–943

From the formal division of Benevento in 849 until the death of Pandulf I Ironhead (943–981) in 981, the Lombard world of southern Italy was the theatre for a series of internecine struggles for dominance from powers sited in the region but also those whose main centres were exterior to the peninsula. Of these protagonists the Islamic contribution has received important attention in recent years, which has reviewed their crucial significance in forming a rounded view of this period. No less important, however, was the increasing role of Byzantium, which for three years (892–895) controlled all of Benevento but thereafter maintained a hegemonic position on the Puglian coast and over time restored control over most of Calabria and into Lucania (modern Basilicata). Lombard polities were divided between Capua, Benevento, and Salerno with periods of formal and informal unification of Capua and Benevento. Traditional narratives of political events of this period rotate around the rivalries and conflicts of Lombard rulers given that this is the imprint which the available primary sources suggest. However, a careful review of events will also permit us to see how the operation of power and authority was both altered and modulated by local and transregional actors.

The formal division of Benevento in 849, which concluded the civil war between Radelchis I of Benevento and Siconulf of Salerno, marks a watershed moment in the Lombard *Mezzogiorno*. Both sets of combatants had used Islamic mercenaries. Erchempert observed obscurely that "an evil plant must be struck down with an evil wedge," perhaps meaning that one group of Islamic warriors should be opposed by another set.[4] Neither Radelchis nor Siconulf, however, could entirely defeat the other despite their use of Islamic combatants. In a story told in the *Chronicon Salernitanum* we read that Radelchis warned his mercenary leader, called Apolaffar, to leave Benevento before the advent of Guy of Spoleto into the city. Apolaffar was, however, found sleeping in the palace, which makes one ponder whether Radelchis was really in secure control of the military forces at his disposal or in fact subservient to them. Erchempert in one particularly lyrical passage references a "Saracen" king whom he called Massar. Massar resided in Benevento and "devastated everything," and also "took no account of the aristocrats of Benevento and harshly whipped them like inept little servants."[5] Beyond Benevento, of course, from at least 847 there were several functioning amirates in the south of Italy: one based in Bari, another in Taranto, and possibly a third on the coast of Calabria. Whilst separate geographically, these amirates com-

4 Berto, *Little History of the Lombards*, 96.

5 Berto, *Little History of the Lombards*, 98.

bined to render the continuance of a Lombard *Mezzogiorno* uncertain. Given the paucity of independent Islamic commentary on this period and region, it is not unreasonable to see that the Lombard elements of Italy were in some existential peril. Such factors help explain the motivations of Louis II in his interventions into the south and, certainly after the Arab sack of Rome in 846, propelled his involvement and formal resolution of the civil war.

In this period, which corresponds with the rule of Louis II, Frankish attention on the south remained sustained, albeit episodic. From a Lombard perspective, the complex array of interests, protagonists, friends, and enemies could be used to their own benefit. The end of the amirate of Bari and the capture of the enterprising amir Sawdān (ca. 857–871) was a potential moment for Benevento to regain the initiative. Sawdān was described as "most dissolute and most wicked" by Erchempert but praised in the Hebrew *Chronicle of Ahrimaaz*. Adelchis of Benevento (853–878) "granted a tribute and some hostages to Sawdān and signed a peace treaty with him," presumably to end the "cruel devastation" that Erchempert describes, which left the country with "no breath of life in it." Erchempert's prose does not (despite an attempt on his part to do so) give an impression that Adelchis was in a strong geo-political position. The events of the summer of 871 only reinforce this. Despite the *damnatio memoriae* of Sawdān by Christian commentators, it is evident that he remained useful for Adelchis in Benevento after his capture by Louis II. Whilst resident in Benevento, Sawdān and others, we are told, prompted Adelchis to imprison Louis whilst he stayed in the city, and they mocked him when he appeared before the Lombards. Adelchis compelled the emperor to swear an oath never to return to Benevento again without permission. Both the *Rhythmus de captivitate Lhuduici imperatoris* and Erchempert express outrage that "the pious holy man" was treated to such "impiety."[6] Well beyond the borders

6 Berto, *Italian Carolingian Historical and Poetic Texts*, 109.

of Benevento, the imprisonment of Louis II had an immense impact and resonance. It prompted a second installation of Louis as king and emperor once he had obtained his freedom, and for some time thereafter Louis remained cautious and reluctant to intervene in the south.

Despite this imprisonment and oath, and even the end of the amirate of Bari, the Lombard polities were not free from outside attention. The need for Frankish assistance in the face of Muslim military activities did not abate. Both the author of the *Rythmus* and Erchempert directly link the events of 871 with a renewed and organized push by Aghlabid forces to intervene on the Italian mainland. Whilst Adelchis may have had some brief room for independent manoeuvre, Benevento, attenuated in terms of territory and resource, was not capable of mounting a renewal of fortunes. Ominously, Adelchis was "killed by his sons-in-law, nephews and friends" and replaced by Gaideris (878–881), the son of Radelagarius, who had ruled immediately before Adelchis. This may be seen as a pivotal moment for the Lombard south, since it highlights the debilitation of Benevento in comparison with other regional powers. Louis II had attempted to capture Taranto, but with the end of Bari this centre acted as a significant element in Islamic military conquest. 'Uthmān, who held the city, was able to orchestrate raids on Benevento, Telese, and Alife and caused such fear as to warrant the inhabitants of Bari inviting the Imperial *baiulos* of Otranto, Gregory, to take over their city. Such development pre-empted the successful Byzantine (re-)conquest of most of the Puglian coast and Calabria in the late 880s, which also saw the occupation of Benevento itself for three years between 892 and 895. This Byzantine presence was to be an enduring feature of the south of Italy until the fall of Bari to the Normans in April 1071. Whilst the population asserted a Lombard identity (indeed, the Byzantine *theme* was named *Langobardia*, for political purposes alone), Puglia was lost to the Lombards. Thus far we have concentrated on events in Benevento, but with the re-calibration of Lombard Italy caused by the Byzantine intervention, the focus of the Lombard world was now restricted to the western, Tyrrhenian side of the peninsula. Three significant rulers in the tenth century are worth considering, for they embody the challenges and opportunities that remained for Lombard rulers in the final centuries of the Lombard *Mezzogiorno*. First, Atenulf of Capua (887–910), who represents the dexterity of Capuan rulers in this period; second, his son Landulf III/I (910–943); and third, Pandulf Ironhead, who unified Lombard lands for one final time, but only under his own personal authority.

Capua had emerged as independent during the civil war between the claimants for Benevento during the ninth century steered by Landulf I. During this period we have the narrative of Erchempert, which dwells sufficiently on Landulf and his relatives, allowing us to see how the family simultaneously participated in the dizzying array of conflicts and violence in this period and also walked a tightrope between Salerno and Benevento. Ultimately, however, Capua solidified its independence, partly by the shared way in which all the *Landolfingi* exercised power. At the same time, this did not mean that there was no dissension or rivalry between the various branches of the family. Atenulf had been Count of Capua from 887, but from 899 he was also Prince of Benevento until his death in 910. His rule was the harbinger of a link between the two provinces that was to endure for most of the tenth and eleventh centuries. A measure of Atenulf's ability can be pinpointed from his appearances in Erchempert's narrative. Here, he first appears as a candidate in the machinations of Athanasius II of Naples (878–898), who sought to enfold Capua under the domination of his city. Rather than adhere to an alliance with Athanasius, according to the story of Erchempert, Atenulf revealed the designs of the Neapolitan ruler to his brothers, and together with all their cousins they continued to oppose Naples. The political intrigue and conflicts which occupy Erchempert's narrative cumulatively depict Atenulf's efforts to assume a primacy in Capua that marginalized his brothers and cousins so that he could attain unopposed rule. Once installed as the sole ruler of Capua, he was ultimately able to acquire Benevento after the latter had been controlled by Constantinople (892–895) and then Guy of Spoleto (895–897).

From this point, Atenulf and his successors maintained a link between Capua and Benevento, said to be "indissoluble." On his death in 910, he passed his authority to his son Landulf I/II without contention. Landulf helped in the construction of an anti-Islamic alliance with nearly all the local powers in the south of Italy, including Amalfi and Naples, who had benefited from trade with the Muslims. Their prime target was the Islamic raiders based at the mouth of the river Garigliano and who in 915 were defeated and expelled. In terms of governance, an imprint of recurring activity may be said to occupy the tenth century. The princes of Capua-Benevento associated their brothers and sons into rulership. Landulf I, for instance, ruled with Atenulf III (936–943) and Landulf II/III (939–943). This approach runs until the last Lombard rulers. Landulf I's prime activities, once the Islamic raiders had been dealt with, were to oppose the Byzantine Empire in Puglia and try to regain a presence on the Adriatic coast, but his attempts to dislodge the Empire from the north of modern-day Puglia were to prove unsuccessful. In 929, for example, despite an alliance with Guaimar II of Salerno (901–946) and Theobald of Spoleto (928–936), a set of incursions into Calabria and Puglia ended without long-term results and in defeat.

A New Arechis? Pandulf Ironhead, 943–981

Barbara Kreutz suggested that the career of Pandulf Ironhead was the beginning of the end of Lombard Italy, but there were no objective reasons for believing that contemporaries of Pandulf would have seen the Lombard world in existential crisis at this point. That said, as we saw with the activities of Landulf I of Benevento, none of the smaller powers in the south were able to dislodge the Byzantine Empire from control of its three local *themes*. Accommodation and contest between the Lombards and the western and eastern empires oscillated throughout the remainder of the tenth century. Pandulf's career marks a new approach to the problem in which

Pandulf's acquisition of control of all three Lombard entities was intertwined with an alliance with the newly minted Ottonian emperors but also involved him in the murky world of papal politics. Previously, Lombard rulers adopted alliances based on expediency. On occasion, rulers would seek formal Byzantine titles and acknowledge Byzantine emperors in dating formulas in charters (as was also the case in the later eighth century with Charlemagne) but essentially remain entirely independent. Pandulf's use of an alliance with the Ottonian emperors to advance his local interests and to oppose Byzantium at least permitted him to re-unite the three Lombard polities under his personal rule, but lacked sufficient institutional depth to survive his demise.

It is difficult, however, to ascribe this reunification as the cornerstone of a long-prepared policy. Initially, Pandulf seems to have been drawn into the networks linked to the Ottonian emperors by his interactions with popes supported by the Ottonians. John XIII (965–972), for instance, escaped imprisonment from a rebellion in Rome and took refuge with Pandulf in Capua. Whilst he resided there, the pope raised Capua to an archdiocese; ten months later, when Otto I (936–973) had crushed the rebellion in Rome, Pandulf sent John back to Rome with a Capuan escort. Subsequently, Pandulf's acquisition of supremacy in Salerno was entirely based on his support for Gisulf I (952–977), whom he restored to power after his deposition by an alliance led by Landulf of Conza in 973. The real power, however, stood with Pandulf, who was able to intrude his son (another Pandulf) into Salerno as prince after the death of Gisulf, who was childless. Both Pandulf's links with John XIII and his activities beyond Benevento, entangled his rule with the Ottonian project to supplant Byzantium in the south of Italy. Otto I made Pandulf *dux* of Spoleto and Camerino and left him in charge of the siege of Bari in 969, but at the battle of Bovino Pandulf was captured and imprisoned in Constantinople. Ultimately, Pandulf's extensive military activities were not to have any long-lasting effects, so far as the Byzantine Empire was concerned. On his death his domains were divided amongst his sons. It may have seemed that the Lombard *Mezzogiorno* had simply returned to business as usual.

Endgame: Poachers Become Gamekeepers, 981–1071

Just as it has proven difficult not to deploy hindsight with the end of the Lombard Kingdom in the north in 774, so too is this the case with the end of Lombard polities in the *Mezzogiorno* in the eleventh century. Here, of course, the Lombards become entirely entangled into narratives which depict the Norman achievement in crafting a new Norman Kingdom of Sicily as almost ineluctable. The actions of the Normans, however, across the period from 999 onwards in assisting, sometimes undermining and ultimately picking off their erstwhile Lombard allies did not constitute a clear and deliberate program of "state" formation. It should perhaps be emphasized at this stage that the Normans did not constitute a simple monolithic block of protagonists and sometimes worked against each other (Figure 6). It is not axiomatic, therefore, that the Normans as actors on the southern Italian political field would become the quintessential poachers turned gamekeepers. Their first recorded interventions, at least according to Amatus of Montecassino (ca. 1015–ca. 1090), whose *Ystoire de li Normani* (*The History of the Normans)*, recounts how the "valiant" Normans, apparently a party of pilgrims, delivered the "citizens of Salerno from the bondage to the pagans" (i.e., the Saracens).[7]

The Norman appearance in the first half of the eleventh century adds a further layer to the geopolitical realities on the ground. This period is a complex one to follow. The array of individuals and interests at stake complicates an already complex landscape. Yet, as Graham Loud points out, so far as the Lombards were concerned, as late as the 1040s there still

7 Prescott N. Dunbar, *The History of the Normans by Amatus of Montecassino* (Woodbridge, 2004), 50.

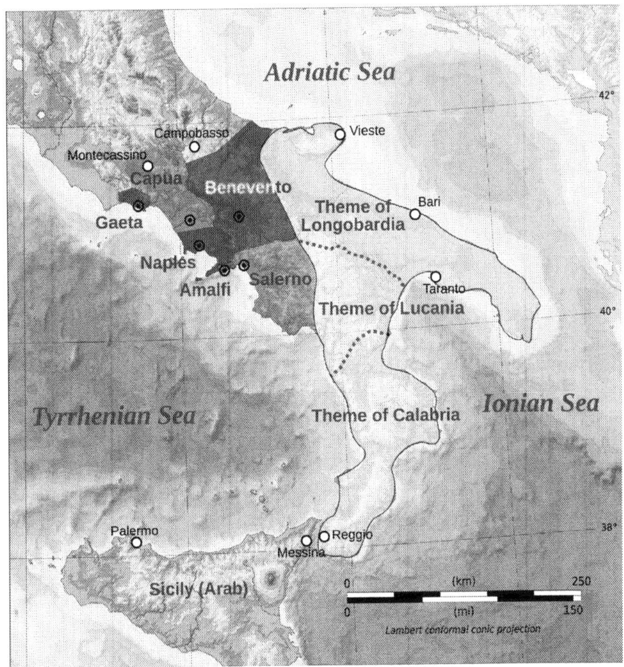

Figure 6. Map of southern Italy around 1000 prior to the Norman impact. Map by Classical Geographer. Wikimedia Commons. CC BY-SA 3.0.

seemed to be a Lombard future as much as a Lombard past. Still pertinent in this period were conditions in Byzantine *Langobardia* and the successors of Otto III (996–1002), as western emperors retained their intermittent interest in the area. Of course, the internal dynamics and strengths of the three Lombard polities should be factored into any equation that tries to explain their ultimate demise. It is a paradox, perhaps, that having "collated" all three of the Lombard polities under his control and added the duchy of Spoleto and Camerino, the death of Pandulf fated Salerno and Capua-Benevento to come into the hands of separate political masters. Both the patterning of political authority and the apparent progressive diminution of the Lombard polities should be considered in concert with the progressive increase of Norman military and then political power. In this way, we may soften any impulse to see the Norman takeover as somehow inevitable. There is a further irony at work at this time, which, having weathered the storms of Frankish, Islamic, and Byzantine attentions, the Lombard polities succumbed to the infiltration of Normans on both military and political grounds. Let us return now to consider the landscape at the death of Pandulf in 981.

On Pandulf's death, his dominions were split amongst his sons. Landulf IV (981–982) ruled Capua-Benevento whilst Pandulf II (981–982) attained Salerno alone. Neither managed to rule for long. The latter was soon supplanted by John II (983–999) who founded a new family of Salernitan rulers that endured until the last ruler, Gisulf II (1052–1077). The usual link between Capua and Benevento was lost, barring a brief restoration between 1008 and 1014. This provides the context for the endgame of the Lombard principalities which appear to have been particularly vulnerable, as indicated by their frequent alliances with local and trans-regional powers. At first the Normans provided additional military muscle for Salerno, which was able to expand at the expense of local powers. In 1038, for instance, a combined Salernitan-Norman army captured Amalfi and four years later went on to acquire large tracts of Puglia. The use of Norman mercenaries in this context, no doubt, made perfect sense to the rulers; it had the benefit of military tradition, but it underestimated the Normans as independent actors and their willingness to "play second fiddle."

Due to the inextricable nature of Lombard polities in this period, it is not possible to provide a narrative that does not involve all three entangled together. That said, there are distinctly different ultimate trajectories, although, given their longevity, the rapidity of their decline is quite surprising. Out of the three domains ruled by Pandulf Ironhead, Benevento proved to be the least robust in the eleventh century. Denuded of access to either the Adriatic or the Tyrrhenian coasts, it was limited to the Apennine uplands and thus at the mercy of opponents on all sides. After Landulf IV's death in 982, Pandulf II (982–1014) became Prince of Benevento. In the customary fashion, Pandulf associated his son Landulf V (987–1033) into his authority, but already from this period its territory had dwindled to the city and its immediate hinterland and had attracted the attention of papal ambitions. Clearly the assumption of control of Benevento by the Papacy was more complicated and protracted than Amatus suggests. He reported that Pope Leo IX (1049–1054)'s visit to the city in 1050 had propelled the citizens of the city to drive out their Lombard rulers due to "the perfection and sanctity of the pope."[8] Thereafter the Lombard rulers ruled as papal vassals until the death of Landulf VI (1059–1077), whose death marked the end of Lombard rule in the city.

Capua's position, if nothing else, had been geographically more favourable than its neighbour Benevento, but it was subject to serious internal instabilities. The murder of Landenulf II (982–993) by his brother Laidulf (993–999) in 993 marked a significant watershed moment. Laidulf was in turn removed from power by the western Emperor Otto III and exiled to Germany and replaced with Adhemar (1000), who was also *dux* of Spoleto. After less than six months, however, he was supplanted. These events demonstrated the inherent weakness of the Lombard polities more generally. Such debilitation was further revealed by their involvement with the Lombard rebel Melus of Bari (d. 1020) and his opponent, the Byzantine *Katepan* Basil Boiannes (1017–1027). This may be said to be the final drama of Lombard Italy. The first revolt of Melus and his brother Dattus (d. 1021) against the Byzantine *Katepan* had been defeated in 1011. Subsequently, Melus encountered the Normans by chance and persuaded them to assist him in further resistance. Byzantine opposition to Melus, his defeat and exile, the construction of a strong line of defence by the Byzantine *Katepan* in northern Puglia, and the execution of Dattus all prompted a military

8 Dunbar, *History of the Normans*, 92.

intervention by the western Emperor Henry II (1014–1024), which served to destabilize the situation in the south further. On his appearance in the south, Henry deposed Pandulf IV "the Wolf" (1016–1022, 1026–1038, and 1047–1050) and exiled him to Germany. When Pandulf finally returned from exile, his injudicious efforts to take revenge for his captivity in Germany progressively undermined Capua's stability and, for that matter, also ensnared Salerno into a constellation of yet more disruption and violence. His successors, Pandulf VI (1050–1057) and his brother Landulf VIII (1057–1058), the last Lombard rulers of Capua, were only left with a principality in disarray that was essentially restricted to the city itself. Thus, when the Norman commander Richard Drengot (ca. 1025–1078), Count of Aversa, besieged Capua and took the city, he ended the independence of the principality (although Landulf was allowed to govern under supervision until his death in 1062).

Salerno had emerged into the eleventh century with the most stable and promising position for the three Lombard states. The careers of Guaimar III (or IV; ca. 994–1027) and his son Guaimar IV (or V; 1027–1052) demonstrate this stability with their impressive tenures as rulers. In all the complicated machinations described above, Salerno still retained a strength to resist external enemies and went on the offensive in the later 1030s/early 1040s, albeit with Norman assistance. Partly due to the accidents of geography but also due to the remarkable longevity of its princes, Salerno was not as exposed as either Capua or Benevento. It was even able to view Byzantine recrudescence on the Puglian coast and even northern Calabria with some circumspection. Guaimar IV was viewed positively by Amatus. He was, he indicated, "possessed [of] all the qualities that a layman should have—except that he took an excessive delight in women."[9] The use of Norman mercenaries to extend Salernitan authority couldn't protect Guaimar from the endemic political violence

9 Dunbar, *History of the Normans*, 96.

of this period, and in 1052 he was assassinated by his relatives. Emplaced under Norman protection, Guaimar's son Gisulf II became prince but harboured an enduring antipathy to his protectors (and indeed relatives) amongst the Norman leaders. Where his father was praised by Amatus, Gisulf was described as a man full of "arrogance, pride, greed, gluttony, avarice," amongst many other faults.[10] Whilst it is evident that Amatus exaggerates, Gisulf's antipathies (and perhaps stubbornness) proved to be his undoing, and in 1076 Salerno was besieged by Richard (Drengot) I of Capua and Robert Guiscard (ca. 1015–1085), Gisulf was exiled and Salerno ceased to exist as an independent Lombard polity.

The slow death of the Lombard polities in the south leads one to the rather sad conclusion that Lombard Italy, politically speaking, ended with a whimper rather than a bang. Yet in truth, as one considers the longer trajectory of resilience across the period from 849 onwards, the Lombards had endured the often-unwelcome attentions of outsiders. Fishing in these troubled waters did not result in solid hegemony for exterior protagonists, but over the longer term it did undermine any efforts to craft or re-craft a Lombard dominion that could emulate the old Beneventan duchy in terms of control of territory and power. Whilst Lombard rulers were often dexterous in their ability to use, for their own purposes, both western and eastern emperors to maintain their freedom, it was often a precarious exercise without long-term guarantees of success. When facing a determined and organized local foe, such as the Normans, who progressively inveigled themselves into the elite networks of the south, the small Lombard polities met opponents they could not resist. Intermingled and married into the Lombard elite networks, the Norman infiltration was only one step away from the creation of a new unified southern polity under Norman auspices. In this sense, the Kingdom of Sicily proved to be the real inheritor of the Beneventan Lombards.

---

10 Dunbar, *History of the Normans*, 123.

Further Reading

Printed Primary Sources

Azzara, Claudio, and Stefano Gasparri, eds. *Le leggi dei Longobardi: Storia, memoria e diritto di un popolo germanico.* Viella, 2005.

Berto, Luigi Andrea, ed. *The Little History of the Lombards of Benevento by Erchempert: A Critical Edition and Translation of "Ystoriola Longobardorum Beneventum."* Routledge, 2021.

Davis, R. *The Lives of the Eighth-Century Popes (Liber Pontificalis).* Liverpool University Press, 2007.

Drew, Katherine Fischer, ed. *The Lombard Laws.* University of Pennsylvania Press, 1973.

Still the only English rendering of the laws, convenient although ready to be updated.

Everett, Nicholas. *Patron Saints of Early Medieval Italy c. 350–800.* PIMS, 2016.

An incomparable and useful set of translated hagiographies.

Foulke, William Dudley, ed. *Paul the Deacon: History of the Langobards.* University of Pennsylvania Press, 1907.

Likewise, the only complete rendering in English of this vital source for the Lombards.

Secondary Works

Lombards

Ausenda, Giorgio, et al., eds. *The Langobards Before the Frankish Conquest: An Ethnographic Perspective*. Boydell, 2009.

A detailed but fundamental analysis of the Lombards up to 774.

Christie, Neil. *The Lombards: The Ancient Longobards*. Blackwell, 1995.

Fundamental for the archaeological and material culture aspects of the Lombards, especially important for analysis pre-568.

Everett, Nicholas. *Literacy in Lombard Italy c. 568–774*. Cambridge University Press, 2003.

A superb discussion of literate practices in Lombard Italy which touches on all aspects of life, governance, and society.

La Rocca, Cristina, ed. *Italy in the Early Middle Ages 476–1000*. Oxford University Press, 2002.

Tabacco, Giovanni. *The Struggle for Power in Medieval Italy: Structures of Political Rule*. Cambridge University Press, 1990.

Wickham, Chris. *Early Medieval Italy: Central Power and Local Society 400–1000*. University of Michigan Press, 1981.

Still very important and packed with insight even after forty years.

Space and Landscape

Balzaretti, Ross. *Dark Age Liguria: Regional Identity and Local Power c. 400–1020*. Bloomsbury, 2013.

Significant work that brings environmental and landscape histories to the forefront of discussion.

Balzaretti, Ross. *The Lands of St Ambrose: Monks and Society in Early Medieval Milan*. Brepols, 2019.

A masterpiece of historical scholarship.

Christie, Neil. *From Constantine to Charlemagne: An Archaeology of Italy 300–800*. Ashgate, 2006.

Christie's overview is an effective and useful treatment of the subject; invaluable.

Panato, Marco. *River and Society in Northern Italy: The Po Valley, 500–1000.* Amsterdam University Press, 2024.

A superb monograph which discusses important economic and societal issues.

Squatriti, Paolo. *Landscape and Change in Early Medieval Italy: Chestnuts, Economy and Culture*. Cambridge University Press, 2013.

All of Squatriti's monographs are valuable discussions of the environmental and social worlds of early medieval Italy.

Squatriti, Paolo. *Water and Society in Early Medieval Italy 400–1000*. Cambridge University Press, 1998.

Ward-Perkins, Bryan. *From Classical Antiquity to the Middle Ages: Urban Public Buildings in Northern and Central Italy*. Oxford University Press, 1984.

Society and Economy

Goodson, Caroline. *Cultivating the City in Early Medieval Italy.* Cambridge University Press, 2021.

Excellent work which provides much food for thought on the socio-economic landscapes of Italy.

Harrison, Dick. *The Early State and the Towns: Forms of Integration in Lombard Italy 568–774*. Lund University Press, 1993.

Wickham, Chris. *Framing the Early Middle Ages: Europe and the Mediterranean 400–800.* Oxford University Press, 2006.

Belief, Law, and Identities

Dunn, Marilyn. *Arianism*. Arc Humanities, 2021.

Szada, Marta. *Conversion and the Contest of Creeds in Early Medieval Christianity*. Cambridge University Press, 2024.

An excellent and up-to-date examination of the religious landscapes of the Mediterranean world after the western Roman Empire.

The Kingdom: Pavia, 568–774

Antonopoulos, Panagiotis. *The Reign of King Cunincpert: Saga, Reality, Stability and Progress in Lombard Italy at the End of the Seventh Century*. Porphyrogenitus, 2010.

Useful study of the rule of Cunincpert in the late seventh century.

Borri, Francesco. *Alboino: Frammenti di un racconto (secoliVI–XI)*. Viella, 2016.

Fabbro, Eduardo. *Warfare and the Making of Early Medieval Italy (568–652)*. Routledge, 2020.

Gasparri, Stefano, ed. *Il Regno longobardo in Italia: Struttura e funzionamento di un stato altomedievale*. CISAM, 2004.

Goffart, Walter. *The Narrators of Barbarian History (A.D. 550–800): Jordanes, Gregory of Tours, Bede, and Paul the Deacon*. Princeton University Press, 1988.

Heath, Christopher. *The Age of Liutprand: Dynamics of Powerin Eighth Century Italy*. Bloomsbury, 2025.

Heath, Christopher. *The Narrative Worlds of Paul the Deacon: Between Empires and Identities in Lombard Italy*. Amsterdam University Press, 2017.

Langobardia Minor: The Lombard *Mezzogiorno* 774–1071

Anderson, Julie. "Historical Memory, Authority, and the Written Word: A Study of the Documentary and Literary Culture at the Early Medieval Court of Benevento, 700–900 CE." PhD Diss., University of Toronto, 2017.

> Superb doctoral thesis which tackles the political and intellectual cultures of Benevento.

Kreutz, Barbara. *Italy Before the Normans: Southern Italy in the Ninth and Tenth Centuries*. University of Pennsylvania Press, 1992.

> Useful as a first introduction to the subject.

Loud, Graham. *The Age of Robert Guiscard: Southern Italy and the Norman Conquest.* Pearson, 2000.

> Loud's immense contribution to Norman Italy is well-known, this synthetic overview does not disappoint.

Ramseyer, Valerie. *The Transformation of a Religious Landscape: Medieval Southern Italy 850–1150*. Cornell University Press, 2006.

> Recounts the religious and socio-cultural landscapes of southern Italy.

Zornetta, Giulia. *Italia meridionale longobarda: Competizione, conflitto e potere politico a Benevento (secoli VIII–IX)*. Viella, 2020.

> This is an important work which provides an up-to-date analysis of the Lombard *Mezzogiorno*.

Printed in the United States
by Baker & Taylor Publisher Services